Living with
Infertility ~
a Christian Perspective

Text copyright © Rosemary Morgan 2013
The author asserts the moral right
to be identified as the author of this work

Published by
The Bible Reading Fellowship
15 The Chambers, Vineyard
Abingdon OX14 3FE
United Kingdom
Tel: +44 (0)1865 319700
Email: enquiries@brf.org.uk
Website: www.brf.org.uk
BRF is a Registered Charity

ISBN 978 0 85746 083 7

First published 2013

10 9 8 7 6 5 4 3 2 1 0

Acknowledgments
Unless otherwise stated, scripture quotations are taken from the Holy Bible, New International
Version (Anglicised edition). Copyright © 1979, 1984 by Biblica (formerly International Bible
Society). Used by permission of Hodder & Stoughton Publishers, an Hachette UK company.
all rights reserved. 'NIV' is a registered trademark of Biblica (formerly International Bible
Society). UK trademark number 1448790.

Extracts from *Common Worship: Services and Prayers* are copyright © The Archbishops' Council
2000, and are reproduced by permission. All rights reserved. copyright@churchofengland.org

The paper used in the production of this publication was supplied by mills that source their
raw materials from sustainably managed forests. Soy-based inks were used in its printing and
the laminate film is biodegradable.

A catalogue record for this book is available from the British Library

Printed in Singapore by Craft Print International Ltd

Living with
Infertility –
a Christian Perspective

ROSEMARY MORGAN

Contents

Foreword 6

Introduction 7

1 Does God understand? 13

2 Anger and blame....................................... 24

3 Hope and despair 48

4 Jealousy.. 63

5 Confusion and decision-making................. 73

6 Disappointment and letting go.................. 93

7 Loving and being loved............................ 107

8 Obsession.. 127

Further resources 134

Notes... 136

Foreword

I married late, on my 36th birthday, and consequently began 'trying for a baby' at an age when fertility is already dramatically decreasing. When nothing happened, I had a severe breakdown with the stress of it all. I wish I'd had this book then. I only had two years of the pain of infertility (although the birth of our 'miracle' son was not the end of our struggles!). For many, infertility is a much longer sentence, perhaps a lifetime one.

In this valuable book, Rosemary Morgan travels that lonely path with women (and men) who long for a child but fear they will never reach the light at the end of the tunnel. With great compassion and down-to-earth advice, she seeks spiritual comfort in the experience of infertility and finds a God who is with us in all our frustration, jealousy, anger and despair.

At last a Christian has written on this subject, on which churches often keep an embarrassed silence. I hope many will find renewed strength, hope and acceptance in this book, and that, as a result, the topic will be one that Christians feel free to talk about.

Veronica Zundel

Introduction

Reading a book can't actually change things. It won't help you to get what you want; nor will it stop you wanting it. But reading a book can help to change us. New ideas and new ways of looking at old ideas can help us to see things from a different point of view. This book attempts to reframe the Christian experience of infertility, to enable you to see it in the context of a wider story of your life with God.

My experience of infertility did terrible things to my relationship with God. I was angry and disappointed; I avoided God.

I remember sitting with another member of my church and hearing him say, 'Adversity can really bring people closer to God. When things are difficult, it can give us a wonderful sense of God's presence with us.' I was furious. I felt no such closeness, only pain. I felt forgotten by God.

It didn't have to feel like that. God was with me even then. God does know the pain of infertility and childlessness. He has been here before us, he is sharing this sorrow with us, and he already knows how this story will end. Your story is also God's story. He is sharing it with you and he is willing to make it into a part of his story.

One of the reasons that I was so angry with God was the presentation of infertility in the Bible. I could only see references to it as something in the past. It was mentioned briefly, merely to emphasise the wonder and miracle of birth. This verse in particular haunted me: 'Then God remembered Rachel; he listened to her and opened her womb' (Genesis 30:22).

This is a verse of celebration. It's about the end of a

long and painful period of infertility. It's about God finally answering the prayer that Rachel had prayed so many times. When I was first struggling to come to terms with my own infertility, this verse seemed to tease me. I couldn't stop thinking about it. God remembered Rachel and he gave her a baby. God listened to Rachel and opened her womb. God wasn't opening my womb, so did that mean he wasn't listening to me? If God didn't give me a baby, did that mean he had forgotten me?

There are several other characters like Rachel, who are blessed with a baby after a long period of infertility. I found their stories painful rather than hopeful. I didn't want to hear about how joyous it was to have a baby; I wanted to hear about how to cope with not having a baby. I didn't want to focus on that moment of celebration, because that wasn't where I was living. I was living in the 'before', and that was what I wanted to talk to God about. I can assure you now that this isn't a book about the moment of celebration. This book is about the sometimes long and frequently painful period of infertility. It is about the time before God 'remembers'. I promise not to spring a surprise 'happy ending' on you. No babies will be born in the course of this book!

When God answers your prayers and opens your womb, when you finally hold that much-wanted baby in your arms, you might find it comforting to think that God has remembered you. But the unfortunate flipside is that if God doesn't seem to hear you, if God doesn't open your womb, if you don't bear a child, you may feel that God has forgotten you. This book is about what to do when you feel that you have been forgotten by God.

The Bible is full of barren women but, when we read it, we often seem to skip ahead to the end, when they have a baby and everything is all right again. That is unfair to barren women and it is unfair to the Bible. The Bible actually has plenty to say about the experience of waiting, of being disappointed, being jealous, angry and unhappy—and, of course, it is packed with advice for difficult times.

Rachel went through years of infertility before she got pregnant. She had to deal with jealousy, disappointment and humiliation. While she was unable to conceive, her sister Leah (who was also married to Rachel's husband) bore several healthy sons. Rachel and her husband had a child through a surrogate. Then, eventually, Rachel herself conceived. Rachel's journey was not simple or short. She struggled and tried several different methods to build her family. She may well have felt abandoned by God, but God was alongside her for every step of her journey.

In reality, God is alongside all barren women all the way through their infertility, and God will stay by your side throughout your experience of infertility too. He never forgot Rachel and he has not forgotten you. This book aims to show how God is alongside us and within us: he suffers infertility with us and goes ahead of us to show us the way forward. We need to refocus our eyes so that we can see God with us.

Infertility is not often a sudden diagnosis. Usually it is discovered gradually, when the expected baby fails to arrive month after month. It takes time to move from vaguely wondering why it is happening (or not happening) to thinking of yourself as infertile. Length of time is frequently used as a tool in diagnosing infertility. In most cases, doctors suggest it only when a certain amount of time has passed. Waiting is not only a big feature of the treatment; it is even part of the diagnostic procedure.

Like being diagnosed with infertility, dealing with infertility is a gradual process. It takes time to accept this new view of ourselves and our world. Nobody is capable of dealing with their infertility all at once. For everyone, it must be a gradual process. There will be new losses, fresh realisations of old losses, and new and deeper disappointments. There may be a period of grief over being unable to give our parents a grandchild, and another period of grief over being unable to have a child christened. Walking past a row of newborn-sized baby vests might bring on a sudden rush of pain, because we have no reason to buy one but desperately want to do so. The pain of infertility comes and goes in waves and sudden showers. It is hard to put it behind us, because it doesn't assault us all at once.

I cannot talk about a time when I first realised I was infertile, because it wasn't like that. Nor can I say that I am writing this book having fully rationalised and come to terms with my own infertility, because that cannot happen. There will always be the possibility of a miracle. Until the day I die, we will not know for sure that I will never bear a child. I am writing this, then, as someone who has experienced, and still does experience, the particular pain of infertility.

This book is not about living through infertility, as though it was a tunnel on the way to the ultimate destination of childbearing. It is about living within infertility, continuing to have a spiritual life, and doing something more than simply sitting around waiting for a baby.

Earlier in my journey of infertility, I looked for a book that would describe a Christian perspective on my situation. I could not find one, so I decided to write the book that I would have liked to have read in those early days. I hope that others who have similar experiences will find it helpful.

I am a lay preacher, which means that I sometimes write

and preach sermons. I found that, while I struggled with infertility, my sermons were often about the struggle to find God when we are in pain. Every time I turned to God in prayer or took up the Bible for study, I found myself looking for answers. I wanted to know why God was allowing me to be hurt, where God was in my experience of infertility. I put my answers into my sermons, and here I have collected them all together into one place. It is a very personal approach and I apologise for the areas that I have not covered. Your experience of infertility will certainly be different from mine; your experience of God will certainly be different from mine. I hope, though, that reading about my experiences will help you to live faithfully through yours.

When my mother read this book, she told me that it made her sad. She didn't like to think that I had been through the moments of despair and rage that this book describes. She also said that it helped her to understand me better, and that the strength of the sorrow taught her how strong had been the consolation that God has given (and still does give) me. I hope that, if you are reading this in order to understand better the feelings of an infertile person that you are supporting, you will see the consolation as well as the despair.

A note on the structure of this book

Each chapter is designed to help you find God beside you within a particular experience. Your journey through infertility will probably carry you through a variety of different emotional states, and I hope you will find a chapter to accompany you in many of them.

The chapters begin with some thoughts that I have had, and some that I have heard other people express during their own times of infertility. I don't record these as examples worthy of emulation, but as milestones to help clarify the state of mind about to be addressed. If the ideas at the beginning of a chapter describe how you are feeling right now, then that is the chapter for you to read right now.

Each chapter goes on to consider the biblical perspective on those feelings and concludes with a short prayer. I hope that these prayers will inspire you to bring your own feelings to God.

CHAPTER 1

Does God understand?

'God has never been a woman.'

'God hasn't tried being barren.'

'I don't think that this sort of thing interests God. I'm not sure that it would seem very important to him.'

'God chooses to bless some people with babies and not others. There's nothing that I can do to influence him either way.'

'I feel guilty when I go to church. I don't want to praise God at the moment; all I want to do is ask him to give me a baby.'

'I thought that suffering was supposed to bring people closer to God, but I just seem to be drifting further and further away.'

Church is supposed to offer us support, a safe place to open up our souls in worship and petition. Sometimes, though, I have found the church to be a terrible place, where lemon juice is poured on my wounds. It feels strange to say that I have plenty of examples of difficult services, where it seemed as though the worship leader (and, thus, by my own personal extrapolation, God) was oblivious of my pain—yet it is true. I have sat through many services wishing that someone understood me, bitterly disappointed not to find that understanding and comfort within the service itself, and distracted from worship by the reminders of my individual concerns.

Advent is often hard, with all the sermons about waiting for a child. When we first began our quest to become parents, my husband and I thought that was what we were doing—waiting for a child. As the quest became longer and the disappointments piled up on top of one another, waiting began to look like the wrong image. We are not waiting any longer. Now we are fighting, mourning, seeking, longing. Waiting for a baby is what we used to do.

Mothering Sunday can be horrendous. Listening to a sermon celebrating the gift of motherhood can be a painful reminder that it is not a gift that I have been given. Watching other people's children give their mothers flowers or cards makes me feel sad. Usually, we skip church on Mothering Sunday. In fact, there have been years when I have found it torturous even to go looking for Mother's Day cards for my mother and mother-in-law. I don't always want to be reminded of the family I haven't got.

The worst times in church, however, have been those unexpected paeans to motherhood. One Christmas, I was visiting a different church from my own. The minister's sermon was thoughtful and beautiful, an intensely personal portrait of the joy of motherhood and birth, describing in great detail his own feelings on seeing his wife holding their young children for the first time. I sat in an unfamiliar pew, with my husband's hand in mine, and wept for the baby that I wasn't holding and for my husband's arms which were still empty of that great gift of a child.

At moments like that, it seemed as though nobody could

possibly understand my pain. It certainly seemed as though God did not empathise with me. How could he? He is the Creator of all. How could he possibly understand the pain of barrenness? How could he who never fails possibly be beside me in my repeated failures?

Well, the church is made up of Christians and so it makes plenty of mistakes. There are plenty of ministers and vicars who do not understand the pain of infertility (although, of course, there are also plenty who do). When I began searching the Bible, however, I began to see that pain and suffering are things that God knows very well indeed. I found not only a God who stands alongside those who suffer but also a God who has suffered. When I looked for him, I found a God who knew very well how it felt to suffer.

God is alongside us in all of our joys and all of our sufferings. He knows what we are feeling; he knows what we are thinking. He knows us more intimately than anyone else.

God knows all about you

As unique individuals, we all have a unique reaction to infertility.

Of course, infertility cannot be exactly hereditary. Your parents, by definition, had a child somehow. I am fortunate enough to be the second of five children. I grew up in a house that often contained a baby. I saw my mother go through three successful pregnancies. All these experiences made me assume that conceiving and carrying a child was going to be easy.

My mother didn't work while we children were young. She devoted herself to taking care of us, developing her career much later in life, when we were older. Being a parent was central to my parents' sense of self. In particular, I remember that they hardly ever left us with babysitters. (It is a bad idea to trust our childhood memories too far, but I recall being babysat only once a year, when my parents went Christmas shopping, and on three 'one-off' occasions, when they were in hospital for the births of my younger siblings.) My mother used to say, 'Why have children if you don't want to spend time with them?' Being a family was vital to my parents, so being a parent has been central to my image of what it means to be an adult. I found it hard to imagine being an adult and not being a parent.

My childhood made my experience of infertility into what it was. I saw infertility in a particular way because of my ideas of adulthood, parenthood and pregnancy. God has known me all my life, and he knew what experiences had formed my worldview and my infertility-view. 'From birth I was cast upon you; from my mother's womb you have been my God' (Psalm 22:10).

God has been with me every step of the way. He has seen every sorrow that I have ever had. He has heard every prayer and every wish that I have ever made. God knows my entire past. It is hard to explain to anyone else quite how you are feeling, but God really does know where I'm coming from, because he came from there alongside me. No other person can ever see things through my eyes, so no other person will ever see things quite the way that I see them. But God lives in me and he can and does look out through my eyes; he knows how the world looks to me.

When we talk, we each mean something slightly different by the words that we use. Whenever I see the number eight it makes me smile because eight is my youngest brother's favourite number. As a very small child he used to greet new people with the strange question, 'What is your favourite number?' He assumed that, since he had one, everyone else he met must also have a favourite number. When I'm shopping and the total comes to '£8.88' or when I park in a multi-storey car park and find myself on the eighth floor, it always makes me smile because eight is a special number to me now and it reminds me of my brother. God shares this connection with me. He knows why eight is special to me.

You might be able to tell your closest friends about some of the words that have special meaning to you, but you will never be able to tell them exactly how you feel about everything. The very words that you use may mean something slightly different to your friends. Even if you could tell them, you know that you could never get the entire contents of your mind into words.

Speech is a very good method of communication, and it is amazing what we can use it for. It is incredible how much we can say to one another—how precise we can be with our language, how powerful our words can be. But there is only One with whom you can communicate fully. There is only One who knows you completely, who knows all your memories and all the connections that your mind makes. Only God knows you utterly and completely.

When I watch soaps on television, I really hate the 'story so far' section that they put at the beginning. I already know what happened last week because I was watching it! I suppose that the makers put it there in case people have forgotten or missed an episode. Watching the 'story so far' section of a soap isn't the same as having watched the previous episode in its entirety. You might be able to pick up on the main thread of the story, but, unless you watched the previous episode, there will be details that you just don't get.

In a way, the most that you can achieve when sharing your experience with other people is to show them the 'story so far' clips of your life. God, however, has been watching all of the previous episodes. When you talk to God, you do not need to fill in the background. You can be yourself with God, because he already knows what you are like. You can jump in and tell him how you are feeling right now and he will understand. He knows what has gone before and you don't need to let him catch up.

God had a body that failed him too

The incarnation is one of the greatest mysteries of our faith. God himself became a person, just like us, and that gives him a great insight into what it's like to be a person. He knows what we go through because he has gone through it himself. Jesus knows what it is like to suffer as a human being. The Bible tells us nothing of Jesus' own feelings about being (we assume) unmarried and childless, so I don't know if his experience in this area caused him sorrow,[1] but he did experience the pain of being failed by his own body. Mark's Gospel tells us:

> Then they led him out to crucify him. A certain man from Cyrene, Simon, the father of Alexander and Rufus, was passing by on his way in from the country, and they forced him to carry the cross. They brought Jesus to the place called Golgotha (which means The Place of the Skull).
> (MARK 15:20B–22)

Usually Roman soldiers would make the victims carry their own cross to the place of execution. If Jesus didn't carry his own cross, it must have meant that he was unable to do so. We know that Jesus' mission on earth was to live in obedience to his Father's will and eventually to die on the cross. In the last moment, when he was completing his task, Jesus' own body failed him. He couldn't carry his own cross. Jesus knows what it is like to be failed by your own body. When we are distressed because our bodies simply will not do what we want them to do, we can be sure that Christ understands our experience.

Most of the time, we don't distinguish between our selves and our bodies. When we fall over, we might say, 'I hurt myself.' It would be very strange to say, 'I hurt my body.' When a part of our body is weak, it can make us feel as though our 'self' is weak, so, when we suffer a serious illness, we may feel that we are fundamentally unsound. It can be hard to see yourself as a whole and functional person when your body is failing you.

I was once speaking to someone about their cancer diagnosis, and they said, 'I never thought of myself as someone who would get this. I've done everything right.' A serious illness is a crisis of identity: it changes the way we see ourselves. It is hard to get used to our new image of ourselves as an infertile person, but it can be of some comfort to remember that Jesus has been there before us. We can take our concerns and our sorrows to him, knowing that he understands where we're coming from.

The human spirit can endure in times of illness,
but a crushed spirit who can bear?
The heart of the discerning acquires knowledge;
the ears of the wise seek it out. (PROVERBS 18:14–15)

In the Proverbs extract above, the first couplet is a despairing one, but the second couplet changes the perspective and balances the despair with hope. Even when the body is sick and the spirit is crushed, the heart can still acquire knowledge and the ears can still seek it. If you are troubled by infertility and you have picked up this book, then you are probably seeking out knowledge. During this time of sorrow, you can still grow in knowledge and wisdom if you continue to seek God. Infertility does not involve all of you. You can continue to rejoice in the parts of you that are working well.

God knows what it's like to long for a child

The longing for a child of your own is an intense feeling. People talk about their biological clock ticking, telling them that it is time for them to have a baby. When you find yourself unable to have the baby that you want, it's as though your biological alarm has gone off. It can be a dizzying awakening to what's wrong with the world. It can suddenly jolt us into realising how unfair life can be, and how much needless suffering goes on all around us.

'O Jerusalem, Jerusalem, you who kill the prophets and stone those sent to you, how often I have longed to gather your children together, as a hen gathers her chicks under her wings, but you were not willing' (Matthew 23:37). These words were spoken by Jesus as he stood on a hillside, looking down over Jerusalem. There is heartfelt intensity here. Jesus doesn't just talk about currently wanting to gather up the people of Jerusalem. He talks about how often he has longed to do so. That experience is common to those who struggle with infertility. It is not a once-experienced feeling; it is not a passing fancy. The longing to have a child comes to us again and again. It is an intense, heartfelt longing. Too many times for me to count, I have longed for a baby.

Jesus has experienced just the same oft-repeated sense of longing. He, like me, is unable to count how many times he has longed to gather his children in his arms. When we are frustrated by the recurrence, yet again, of our desperate longing for children, Christ will understand how we feel. He too has been struck to the heart by the reappearance of the same old longing.

The image that Christ calls upon here is one from the natural world. He doesn't talk about himself as a mother, but as a hen. I think this is another link to the experience of infertility. The desire to have a child is a primal, animal instinct; the longing to reproduce reminds us of our animal nature. It is a basic desire, coming from the very root of our being. It is not about society or about intellectual thoughts and aims. It is an animal desire to have and to protect our own young. In a similar way, Jesus' desire to gather and protect his children is a strong instinctive desire at the very core of his being.

Finally, Christ acknowledges his own inability to make his desires happen. We are unable to make ourselves have children. Having chosen to give people free will, God has put himself in the position where he can long for his children to come to him, but he will not enforce his will on them. He created the possibility for himself to feel unfulfilled longing. Determined to let people choose for themselves, Christ is unable to make his children return to him. Like us, he is longing without any way of forcing the world to conform to his desire.

In Christ, who became fully human with all the frailties of humanity, God experienced a longing that he could not fulfil. Christ longs for the children of Jerusalem, but he cannot make them his. He cannot force everyone to turn to him of their own volition. He does not demand that Jerusalem turn to him; he does not rain down fire on them until they give in. He does not offer them riches and miraculous health to tempt them to come to him. He accepts that the people of Jerusalem have chosen not to be his children. Although he is God, Christ accepts a world in which things do not happen as he wants them to. Although he is God, Christ accepts the thwarting of his will.

In Christ, God made himself understand what it feels like to want something and not to have it. That is an amazing thing for God—who is all-powerful and self-sufficient—to have done. It is amazing that God, who has everything, should give it all up and become a human being. It is amazing that God, who cannot be hurt, should become a person and suffer pain.

It is amazing that God should suffer longing in the person of Christ—and it is wonderful. Because Christ has felt longing and pain and sorrow, we can feel sure of his empathy. He knows what it is like to long. He has felt the pain of empty arms. He has accepted the things that he doesn't like but cannot change. When we are longing, when our arms ache with emptiness, when we need to learn how to accept what we cannot change, we can look to Christ. He has gone before us and he will lead us on.

We do not need to describe our pain to God in prayer (although we certainly can try to do so, if that helps us). God knows about our pain. He knows what it is like to feel our pain, and he feels it again with us. The Holy Spirit dwells within all who have submitted themselves to Christ and become a part of God's family on earth. The Holy Spirit will intercede with us: if we run out of words to pray, the

Holy Spirit will pray for us. If we cannot express our pain and sorrow, we can just sit in God's presence and the Holy Spirit will speak through our groans, our tears and even our silence (Romans 8:26). We can sit with God, with or without words, and know that he is fully in tune with us.

God will meet us all where we are. He is not afraid to be with us in our suffering. He is not afraid to be with us in our pain. He is not afraid to share our feelings of disappointment and despair. He will meet us here, in the midst of our sorrow, and he will teach us about his nature and his wisdom. As we learn more and more about the wisdom of God, we may even be able to trust him to do what is best for us in our search for children.

Father God, I am not alone.
I am with you and you are with me.
You are going through this experience with me.
You have been by my side, and living within me,
every step of the way.
You will remain with me, always.
Please help me to remember that.
It would be nice if I could feel you with me sometimes.
Please help me to know that you are here.
I know that you understand what it is like to be human,
to be in pain, to be miserable and disappointed.
When I next feel that way, please remind me
that you are feeling it with me. Amen

✳ CHAPTER 2 ✳

Anger and blame

'I'm just so furious all the time.'

'It isn't fair and it isn't right!'

'Other people seem to get pregnant so easily, without even trying. People have babies that they don't want and can't care for properly, and here am I unable to have one that I want so much!'

'My mother-in-law rang up to tell me that yet another cousin was pregnant and I threw the phone across the room. It hit the wall and smashed into pieces. Now, I have no baby and a broken phone.'

'What's wrong with me? Why am I so irritable?'

'When my friend had a miscarriage, a part of me was glad that I didn't have to listen to pregnancy talk any more. Why has infertility turned me into a selfish monster?'

It is safe to say that I felt very angry about my infertility. I was angry with myself. I was angry with my husband and I was angry with God.

A lot of the time, I was sure that the infertility was all my fault. I don't have a pure and perfect past. I have done all sorts of things that I shouldn't have done, things that I am too ashamed to write about.

Sometimes I wondered whether I deserved to have a baby at all. Sometimes, I was so furious with myself for getting into this situation that I hated myself. I stopped buying new clothes, stopped getting haircuts, stopped doing anything that might be considered 'treating myself', because I was so angry with this useless, sinful, barren body of mine. Various books about getting pregnant recommend cutting out caffeine and alcohol, and this suited me. Giving up things that I liked seemed a reasonable price to pay for failing to bear children.

I needed to forgive myself.

There were other times when I blamed my husband for the situation. I picked on him for not caring enough about our lack of children. I nagged him to 'feel' more, to be 'more supportive' (without really knowing what kind of support I wanted). I became angry and demanded to know why he hadn't 'given' me a baby yet.

I needed to forgive my husband.

I was furious with God for refusing to give me a baby. My anger built up inside me, fuelled by every sight of another pregnant woman or a baby in a pram. I directed my anger at God. I was certain that he could give me a baby if he so chose, so I blamed him for my sorrow: he was deliberately choosing to deny me the one thing that I wanted most.

I needed to forgive God.

At my church, I took the oldest Sunday school class—a group of young adults aged 11–16. Each week we read a Bible story together, then I led them in a discussion about the story. One week, I opened the teacher's notes to find that I was going to be talking about the story of Hannah. Hannah, who begs God for a baby and then gets one. The same Hannah who gives her baby back to God, sending

Samuel to live in a church. That Hannah. I was furious. It felt as though God was teasing me. Wasn't it enough to withhold a family from me? Did he have to mock me as well?

I led the study, talking about Eli's callousness, how he assumes that Hannah is drunk because she is so upset. I went home, still furious, too angry to pray. I blamed God and took offence, as if I thought that he was a human like me, deliberately annoying me. It's absurd, of course, but I tried to give the Creator of all things, my own Saviour, the silent treatment. I'm not sure how God felt about my tantrum. I know that all it did for me was to make me feel lonely.

The outbursts of anger didn't help at all. I was left with emotional mess to clear up, and still no baby. What did help, though, was forgiving God. Bear with me: I am aware that forgiving God doesn't sound much better than giving him the silent treatment. But, as a reframing of my thoughts, it was helpful and it brought me back to the Bible.

My anger has been unreasoning and unreasonable. It is not my husband's fault. It is not God's fault. It is not my fault. My infertility is not anyone's fault. It merely exists. I have no good reason to feel angry, but that hasn't stopped me. The only way that I have been able to let go of my anger has been to forgive, even when I am not sure what fault I am forgiving. I have found forgiveness to be the best antidote for anger.

The way that I see it, forgiveness follows three steps: recognition, decision and acceptance. Using these steps has enabled me to forgive myself, my husband and God for my infertility. This is how I let go of the intense anger and stopped wanting to destroy innocent phones.

Recognition

There is a passage in 2 Samuel in which Michal is punished with infertility because she mocks and despises David. The story seems to make it very clear that infertility can be a punishment for sin. Michal sins in her pride when she scolds David for his eager worship of God. By immediately referring to Michal's barrenness, the narrator links the two events and implies strongly that Michal's infertility is the consequence of her despising David. Without stretching your mind and the natural reading of this story, it is hard to come away with any impression other than that infertility is a punishment from God.

It took me a while to realise why this story made me so angry. Now I know: it's because I was afraid that this story confirmed that my infertility was all my fault. If Michal was punished with infertility, then infertility is a punishment. I am infertile, so it must be my fault—some great punishment from God.

'Fault' is not really a very helpful word when discussing the medical reasons for infertility, but I found it to be a word that was very much in my mind and on my lips. When we discovered that it was hard for us to conceive, my husband and I talked about whose 'fault' it might be. When we went to the doctors for various tests, we worried about what might be found out about either of us. I worried that my husband would blame me and he worried that I would blame him. Neither of us wanted to feel that we had inflicted infertility on the other.

Of course your physical abilities and inabilities are not your fault in any true sense of the word. Even if you are not able to have a child because your body is incapable of conceiving or bearing a child to term, it does not mean that your infertility is your fault. Not really. You probably already know this, but it may be much harder for you to feel it.

I wondered frequently whether I would have found it easier to conceive if I had started earlier. I wished we hadn't delayed trying to start our family. When we did delay, of course, we thought that we were doing it for the best of reasons. We wanted to be married before we started our family. We wanted to have a certain amount of financial security. Later, I remembered a friend in the office where I worked telling me, 'There's an old saying: the money comes with the baby.' She meant that there's never a good time to start a family, nobody ever has 'enough' money, but people start families anyway and they usually make do well enough. We thought that we were being sensible and responsible when we delayed starting our family, but I regretted it later and worried that I might have wasted my 'fertile window'.

Paul writes to the Romans:

As it is written: 'There is no one righteous, not even one; there is no one who understands, no one who seeks God. All have turned away, they have together become worthless; there is no one who does good, not even one.' 'Their throats are open graves; their tongues practise deceit.' 'The poison of vipers is on their lips.' 'Their mouths are full of cursing and bitterness.' 'Their feet are swift to shed blood; ruin and misery mark their ways, and the way of peace they do not know.' 'There is no fear of God before their eyes.'

Now we know that whatever the law says, it says to those who are under the law, so that every mouth may be silenced and the whole world held accountable to God. Therefore no one will be declared righteous in his sight by observing the law; rather, through the law we become conscious of sin. But now a righteousness from God, apart from law, has been made known, to which the Law and the Prophets testify. This righteousness from God comes through faith in Jesus Christ to all who believe. There is no difference, for all have sinned and fall short of the glory of God, and are justified freely by his grace through the redemption that came by Christ Jesus. God presented him as a sacrifice of atonement, through faith in his blood. He did this to demonstrate his justice, because in his forbearance he had left the sins committed beforehand unpunished—he did it to demonstrate his justice at the present time, so as to be just and the one who justifies those who have faith in Jesus. (ROMANS 3:10–26)

There is nobody who is perfect, nobody who has never sinned (apart from Christ). I have certainly sinned. Even today, I have done things that I regret and failed to do things that I ought to have done (and, as I write this, it is only ten o'clock in the morning).

If you are to forgive yourself, you must first acknowledge that forgiveness is necessary. I think that people sometimes make the mistake of thinking that forgiveness means ignoring sins. I do not see how that can be the case. If you didn't know that someone had done something wrong, how could you possibly forgive them? You (reading this at some distance from me) do not know what it is that I did wrong today, so you cannot possibly forgive me for it. How can you forgive yourself if you pretend not to know what you did wrong?

There's no point in thinking that we're all right really, or not as bad as so-and-so down the road. It won't even do to compare ourselves with our former selves, thinking we may be a bit short-tempered now, but at least we've improved on what we were like five years ago. That isn't the point. The only true yardstick of goodness is God himself, and we don't measure up very well to him. We must compare ourselves with God, not with other people or with our own personal best. When we compare ourselves with God, we see how flawed we really are.

Before you can forgive yourself, you must acknowledge what you have done wrong. This might involve making a list, either on paper or in prayer to God. There may be something that you suspect has contributed to your infertility, for which you need to forgive yourself, but it may not be anything as clear as that. In the Bible story, Michal was punished with infertility because she was proud. You may also feel that your infertility is a punishment for some past sin.

You might think that God is refusing to give you a baby because you're not a good enough person. If you think that, you should consider what it is that makes you think of yourself as a bad person. What have you done that you think you should not have done? What character traits do you have that you dislike? It is easy to despair if you just think of yourself as a 'bad person' in general. If you are going to forgive yourself, you need to be more specific. You need to think about the details of what it is that you need to forgive.

At first it may hurt you more to think about the parts of yourself that you dislike, but hiding from them won't make them go away. Although it is not a pleasant experience, viewing yourself as you really are is an important experience. You cannot forgive yourself for 'everything that I've ever done wrong': that is far too general. You may even find that it is too general to think of 'all the times that I have been selfish'. You need to be specific, because that is the only way to get real.

When we generalise, we blur the focus and manage to make things seem less real. Wedding photos are often taken in 'soft focus', which blurs the edges, making the surroundings look prettier and even a little unreal. Sometimes I think we are tempted to view ourselves with a mental 'soft focus'. We blur the edges of our actions so that the details disappear. We say, 'I was a bit snappish yesterday because I was very tired.' That makes it sound like a very minor fault. We don't say, 'I went to bed too late because I was watching TV. Then I shouted at my husband in the morning because I was still tired. I yelled at him for brushing his teeth when I wanted to use the bathroom. Then I sulked until we both left the house because I couldn't bear to back down and apologise.' The second story has a lot more detail and describes much more unpleasant behaviour. No wonder we prefer the brief 'soft focus' version of our lives. In order to accept the reality of who we are and what we are like, we need to look at the details.

Spend a bit of time bringing your sin into sharp focus so that you can see what it really is, but don't spend too long on this step. You need to move on to the next steps if you are going to forgive yourself. It may be helpful to write things down, to say them aloud to God, even to share them with someone whom you trust. The point is to acknowledge that you have done specific things wrong and then know not only that God forgives you but also that you are free to forgive yourself.

Forgiving others is exactly the same as forgiving yourself. First you have to identify the incidents that caused you to blame other people in the first place. If you don't know why you are angry with your partner, you cannot forgive them.

Husbands, love your wives, just as Christ loved the church and gave himself up for her to make her holy, cleansing her by the washing with water through the word, and to present her to himself as a radiant church, without stain or wrinkle or any other blemish, but holy and blameless. In this same way, husbands ought to love their wives as their own bodies. He who loves his wife loves himself. After all, no one ever hated his own body, but he feeds and cares for it, just as Christ does the church—for we are members of his body. 'For this reason a man will leave his father and mother and be united to his wife, and the two will become one flesh.' This is a profound mystery—but I am talking about Christ and the church. However, each one of you also must love his wife as he loves himself, and the wife must respect her husband. (EPHESIANS 5:25–33)

When Paul wrote this passage, he was taking it for granted that everyone must love themselves and their body. We must love ourselves first, before we know what it would mean to love someone else. Before even that, we must know what it is to be loved. First we must accept love and forgiveness from God; then we can learn to love and forgive ourselves. Once we have done this, we can learn to love and forgive others. Paul tells husbands to love their wives 'as themselves', assuming that they have already mastered loving themselves. If we can forgive ourselves, then, surely we should be able to forgive our partner. If we love them as we love ourselves, then forgiving them should be both as easy and as difficult as forgiving ourselves.

Do you blame your partner for your infertility?

The obvious (and seemingly 'correct') answer to that question is 'No'. We are well aware that it is unfair to blame someone for their medical problems and that it is absurd to blame them for someone else's medical problems. Although you may know perfectly well that it isn't your partner's fault that you are having trouble starting a family, you may still feel unaccountably angry with them. Blame is a natural response to anger and stress. Your partner is close to you and that makes them a likely target for your blame.

However, once you start blaming your partner, it can be hard to stop. Blaming other people is fun and easy and it can make us feel good. If we focus on how badly someone else behaves, it can stop us feeling guilty about our own bad behaviour.

People who suffer are not necessarily more guilty than people who do not suffer. We all know this in our minds, but it can be hard for us really to believe it. Deep down, we want to believe that people suffer because of the wrong they have done. This explains suffering and it makes the world seem like a just and fair place.

The problem arises when we ourselves are the ones who are suffering. Then it is no longer comforting to believe that suffering is the direct result of sin. We end up hating ourselves or hating those who are close to us. If you have been told that there is something medically wrong with your partner that is preventing your conceiving a child together, you are very likely to feel anger towards your partner. This is not a pleasant feeling. You probably realise that you are being unfair and irrational. In order to prevent your marriage from suffering, however, you may well wish to address these feelings.

The first stage is to acknowledge your feelings. If you are going to deal with your emotions, you must recognise them for what they are. Getting angry with your partner a lot more often than usual, wanting to get away from them, getting angry about things that would not normally annoy you—all of these may be signs that you are angry with your partner. If you find that when your partner is happy, you become angry, then it is time to recognise your anger.

Even if it is not really your partner's fault, you may still need to forgive them. It may sound silly to forgive someone when they haven't done anything wrong, but forgiveness is an internal process. Forgiving others is mainly about dealing with your own emotions towards them. It may have nothing to do with the other person at all.

For example, if your house has been burgled, you need to forgive the burglar, even if you never met them, even if they were never caught. You would not be forgiving because you thought it was acceptable or reasonable for them to have burgled your house. You would be forgiving them because it sets you free and enables you to get on with your life.

It is possible to forgive someone who hasn't done anything wrong, if you are angry with them. Forgiveness is the way we deal with resentment, regardless of how that resentment was built up. So do not pretend that you're not angry with your partner, simply because you don't think you ought to be angry like that. If you feel anger, recognise that anger is what you are feeling.

You may wish to consider why you are angry. Are you angry because your partner has actually done something that makes it harder for you to have children? Is there an action in their past for which you need to forgive them? Are you angry because they are not suffering as much as you are? Do you need to forgive them for being able to feel joy when you cannot? Are you angry at the way in which they have handled your stress and sorrow? Do you need to forgive them for not taking better care of you? This is not the best time to consider whether your anger and its extent are justified. Just try to understand your own feelings and thoughts. Try to recognise what you are feeling.

Keeping the focus on our own feelings means that we may choose to forgive our partner for something that they did by accident. We don't need to know their intention in order to forgive them. We are forgiving in order to let go of our own bitterness. It is more important to note our own hurts than it is to establish the degree of intent behind those hurts. If we are going to move on from our pain and bitterness, we need to catalogue what caused that pain and bitterness, but we don't need to catalogue anyone else's actions.

Since it is possible to forgive one who has not deliberately hurt you, it is also possible to forgive God. God has not really hurt you, but you may still feel that he has done so. Here is part of the story of Rachel and Leah:

> Jacob lay with Rachel also, and he loved Rachel more than Leah. And he worked for Laban another seven years. When the Lord saw that Leah was not loved, he opened her womb, but Rachel was barren. Leah became pregnant and gave birth to a son. She named him Reuben [like the Hebrew for 'He has seen my misery'], for she said, 'It is because the Lord has seen my misery. Surely my husband will love me now.' (GENESIS 29:30–32)

Passages like this certainly support anyone who wishes to claim that God could, if he wished to do so, make us all bear children. Leah certainly believed that God chose who should have a baby and when. The narrator obviously believed that it was God who made people fertile or infertile. If you believe this too, then you may well be angry with God for 'choosing' not to give you a baby.

If God saw Leah's misery and gave her a baby, why doesn't he do the same thing for me?

I imagine that Rachel must have been furious with God. He gave a baby to her sister and yet he didn't give one to her. In Rachel's position, I would have felt very angry with God. It would have seemed as though he was taunting me. Yet the Bible does give us a tiny insight into God's mind. It tells us that God gave Leah a baby 'when the Lord saw that Leah was not loved'. God's blessing of Leah with a child was all about God's relationship with Leah; it had nothing to do with God's relationship with Rachel.

When God chooses to bless another family with a child, it is all about God's relationship with that family. It is not about God's relationship with you or with me. If you're angry with God for blessing other couples with children, you may wish to look at Chapter 4 in this book, on jealousy. God did not give Leah a baby in order to upset Rachel. He did it because he loved Leah and could see that a baby was what she needed. We have to trust that the waiting that God planned for Rachel was what she needed as well. God's plans are intended for the good of all.

There is plenty of precedence for people getting angry with God: the Psalms contain many examples. If you find it difficult at first to share your emotions with God, you might find it helpful to read Psalms like 13, 22, 42 and 77. Looking at the psalmists' anger towards God might help you to feel free enough to express your own anger towards him.

You are allowed to be angry with God. Feeling angry isn't the problem and it isn't a sin. Holding on to your anger or allowing your anger to lead you into bad decisions is a problem and a sin. If you are angry with God, recognise it and deal with it. If you need to forgive God for hurting you, then do so. Whatever the rights or wrongs of it, you are angry with God, and forgiving God will enable you to let go of that anger.

Decision

If you have deliberately done something wrong, then you do not deserve to be forgiven. You cannot earn the right to be forgiven by being sorry. I am sure that you are perfectly capable of providing a sincere-sounding apology; however, saying 'sorry' cannot force forgiveness. Equally, no degree of feeling sorry will change what has happened. In fact, one could argue that feeling sorry for doing wrong is proof that you knew it was wrong in the first place and therefore shouldn't have done it! If you didn't know that something was wrong, you cannot be blamed for doing it, but if you did know—indeed, were so sure it was the wrong thing to do that, having done it, you were racked with guilt—then you are fully culpable.

Romans 3:24 (included in the passage quoted earlier) explains that forgiveness comes 'freely' and 'by grace'. There can be no strings attached; there can be no conditions. You forgive yourself because you have decided to do so. You do not need to 'earn' forgiveness by suffering. You don't have to deny yourself a treat or make yourself do something unpleasant. You don't have to 'earn' forgiveness by feeling a certain level of guilt. You don't have to feel guilty 'enough' to be forgiven, either by God or by yourself.

Forgiveness is a gift. It is a gift that we can give others or ourselves, or a gift that we receive. It doesn't matter if you have done something terrible or something slightly naughty. It doesn't even matter how much you regret what you did. You have decided that you will forgive: you will not hold this past mistake against yourself any more. You will not think of yourself as 'the person who did X' or even as 'the kind of person who would do Y'. You are you. You have done some things that you should not have done, and you forgive yourself. You have decided to move on. You will not punish yourself any more.

God is our model. He forgives us and he forgets our sins. Colossians 3:13 commands, 'Forgive as the Lord forgave you.' We can forgive ourselves and forget our sins. If God is content to forget my sins and move on, how much more should I be willing to do so? I certainly cannot claim to have higher standards than God himself. If he is prepared to forgive and forget, it is all right for me to forgive and forget as well.

Forgiveness is the act of letting go of your anger. It means giving up any right that you may have had to vengeance. It means choosing not to attack someone because they have hurt you. However, to forgive does not necessarily mean to protect from just punishment. Even God himself—whose mercy is more complete and pure than ours—does not say that our forgiveness of another will necessarily preclude divine retribution. If we forgive someone who has hurt us, we are not 'letting them get away with it'; we are letting ourselves get away from it. We are not freeing other people to be as depraved as they wish; we are freeing ourselves from having to carry a painful grudge for ever.

If the person we are forgiving is our partner, it is likely that we would wish to free them as well as ourselves. Presumably you wish your marriage to be a good one and the relations between yourself and your partner to be as pleasant and easy as possible. This is all the more reason to determine that you will forgive them for the hurt (whether intentional or not) that they have done to you.

Basically, all blame is the same. Whether we are blaming someone who is really guilty or blaming someone whom we falsely suspect, our feelings are exactly the same. So we are able to blame God, even though he is all goodness; and we are able to forgive him, even though he has never sinned.

You need not understand or excuse God's behaviour in order to forgive it. That is a big advantage, since you are unlikely to understand God's behaviour. I do not know why it is that God should not give me the baby I so earnestly desire, and I do not know why he should withhold that great blessing from anyone who wants it. I cannot imagine why it would be the case that my having a child would not be the best possible situation. I cannot see a single problem that might arise if I were to have a normal pregnancy followed by the birth of a healthy baby. But I do not need to know this.

I have chosen to forgive God for not giving me the baby that I want. I have decided to let go of my anger and blame.

The story of Job is often held up as a source of comfort to those who are suffering. It shows a man who gets furious with God and then manages to forgive God for allowing him to be hurt. Job had been a godly man; he had tried to follow the law; he had reason to believe that he was living as God wanted him to live. Then, suddenly, God gave permission for him to be afflicted with intense sorrows and pains. Job lost his children and became very ill.

I was a Christian for a long time before I began to struggle with infertility. I determined to follow God's way when I was 11 years old. I was baptised at 13. I have led a life littered with coffees served, Sunday school classes taught, Bible studies led and sermons preached. I thought that I had a good relationship with God. I made a lot of mistakes, but it always seemed as though God was there to pick me up again. Then, I found God denying my request for a baby. My desire became more intense and God's response never changed. I began to feel that God was not dealing fairly, that he had not kept faith with me.

What can we do if we think God has wronged us? To whom can we go for restitution? There is nobody who can judge between us and God. If God were to abuse his position and sin against us, we would be defenceless. That is what troubles Job: 'If only there were someone to arbitrate between us, to lay his hand upon us both, someone to remove God's rod from me, so that his terror would frighten me no more' (Job 9:33–34).

Job longs for someone who will rescue him from God's anger, someone who will ensure that God treats him fairly. He complains that God has wronged him and that he has no place in which to appeal.

In Shakespeare's *King Lear* (Act 4, Scene 1) Gloucester laments that the gods treat humans as boys treat flies, killing them for sport. That is not the Christian view of divinity. We are not helpless toys of our God. Christ will speak for us. He is the advocate for humanity. God takes us seriously and agrees to hear our case. John tells us that Christ will be our advocate: 'My dear children, I write this to you so that you will not sin. But if anybody does sin, we have one who speaks to the Father in our defence—Jesus Christ, the Righteous One' (1 John 2:1). We are not defenceless in front of a capricious God. God's own Son, Jesus Christ, will defend us and speak for us.

Never forget that God chose to reply to Job's complaints (Job 38:1). He did not ignore or dismiss Job's concerns; he didn't say that Job had no right to talk to him. God heard Job out. He listened to Job's anger and sense of betrayal, and he will listen to yours too. You can approach God and share your feelings with him, even if you are feeling angry with God himself. He will hear you and heal you better than any human can.

Acceptance

Acceptance is the moment of moving away from sin and getting on with living. At the same time, I know that I am a sinner and I know that I will sin again. Then I will go back to the beginning. Once again I will acknowledge my sin, ask God for forgiveness and find myself back home. The cycle of recognition, decision and acceptance will continue until the end of time, when Christ will somehow perfect me and I will no longer stand in need of his forgiveness. But the repetition of the cycle is no reason to get stuck. You are forgiven once you have asked for forgiveness, and you need to let go of your guilt and move on. This is the final stage of forgiveness.

It is all very well to say that you will forget the past but, in reality, the past is what makes the future. Let us suppose, for example, that a friend breaks a vase that belongs to you. Once you decide that you will forgive your friend for breaking the vase, your friendship will continue as it did before the breakage. You will not talk about your friend's having broken your vase any more, and the event will be forgotten. However, if you also forget that the vase is broken and try to fill it with water and flowers, you will get water all over the floor. What you must do is forget that your friend broke the vase, but remember that the vase is broken.

When we are talking about broken vases, the process is obvious. Who would be so callous as to repeatedly berate a friend for having broken a vase? Who would be so foolish as to try to fill a broken vase with water and use it to display flowers? When your sin hasn't broken a physical vase but has broken an invisible relationship, it is harder to see what has happened. When what you have broken is trust, it can be tempting to try to carry on as before and pretend that there is no need to repair the trust that you have broken.

Forgiving isn't about pretending. It is about stopping the pretence and seeing the reality. You cannot complete the process of forgiveness if you pretend that the sin hasn't happened. Forgiveness is not naïve or weak. It is the action of a strong person who is able to cope with reality. Moving on doesn't mean brushing events under the carpet and pretending they never happened. That isn't what God does with our sin and it isn't what we should do either. God helps us to learn from our mistakes, using them to teach us and mould us into the people he wants us to be. Most importantly, God works with what he's got, not with what he wishes he had. God knows what reality looks like. He knows if the vase is broken, and he would never pretend that it wasn't. Sin has consequences and it is not godly to pretend otherwise.

The third stage of forgiving yourself is to accept the situation that you have created. See what has happened. Is there someone who is suffering because of you? Do you have money that rightfully belongs to someone else? Look around and see the reality of your situation. This is not a time to berate yourself for what you have done. Remember that you have made the decision to forgive yourself. You cannot undo the past but you may be able to improve the future.

Forgiveness is not an easy option. It is about being realistic and sensible. It is about being kind to yourself and to others, and it is about getting on with your life as best you can. If you have forgiven yourself for not taking care of your body, you may now need to look at the condition that your body has reached. Is there anything you can do to improve that condition? This is the time to listen to the advice of a doctor.

God's forgiveness of you and your forgiveness of yourself can undo the damage that your sin has done to your own soul and character. You may be able to undo some of the damage that you have done to other people and to the world around you. There may, however, be some damage that remains. There may be some scars that you cannot erase.

Let us take a small example. Imagine that, feeling a bit lazy, you don't bother to recycle your weekend newspaper. Instead you throw the newspaper into your bin. If you regretted this action before the bins were collected, you could go through the rubbish, recover your newspaper and put it in the recycling bin instead. If you don't regret your action until after the bins have been collected, there is nothing you can do. That newspaper will not be recycled; it will go to landfill. You cannot run after the bin men and demand that they go through all the rubbish so that you can retrieve the newspaper that you have thrown away.

It's just like that with a hurtful comment made to a friend. If you regret a comment as soon as you make it, you can take it back straight away and it may not do any damage. If you wait, however, and try to take back your hurtful comment several days later, it might not be possible. All the hurtful comments and the good comments that your friend has heard will be mixed up in their mind. It will be hard for them to sort through all the baggage that they are carrying, to isolate the single patch of hurt that you caused. It may even be impossible. Sometimes you cannot undo the bad effects that your sin has had on other people. There is nothing to be gained from hanging on to this, however. We have to trust in God's forgiveness, forgive ourselves, and go home.

It will remain the other person's choice whether or not to forgive you. Even if you are able to undo all the damage that you have done, they do not have to forgive you. But, ultimately, you do not need other people's forgiveness. We do not need to be forgiven; we only need to forgive. Our job is to forgive others, not to ensure our forgiveness by others. There is only so much that you can do towards making things right with people whom you have hurt. Their decisions belong to them alone and you cannot force others to choose to forgive you. You can only choose to forgive yourself.

No amount of unforgiveness from others will bring your guilt back into the mind of God, though. It need not bring guilt back into your own mind, either. If you have apologised, you need not continue to brood on your sin. You do need to accept the consequences of your sin, but you no longer need to hold on to those consequences. You can move on and try to make things right. You can concentrate on the future and stop dwelling in the past.

Just as we are tempted to believe that saying the words 'I am sorry' encompasses all that it means to repent of an action, so we are tempted to believe that saying the words 'I forgive you' encompasses all that it means to forgive. We should remember that words are not actions!

In his first letter to the Corinthians, Paul wrote, 'Love is patient, love is kind. It does not envy, it does not boast, it is not proud. It is not rude, it is not self-seeking, it is not easily angered, it keeps no record of wrongs' (1 Corinthians 13: 4–5). He did not write that love '*says* it will keep no record of wrongs', simply that it keeps no such record. We don't need to tell someone that we forgive them in order to do so; it is not necessary for them to accept our forgiveness in order for us to have forgiven them. There may well be cases where it would be desirable for you to tell someone that they are forgiven, and there may be cases where it would be desirable for you to hear them accept your forgiveness. But that is another matter, which has nothing to do with your internal act of forgiveness.

What does it mean to 'accept' that you have forgiven your partner? It means almost exactly the same as it means to accept your forgiveness of yourself. It means to take stock of the situation as it now stands and to move forward from there. There is no need any more to consider whose fault the current situation may be. You are looking merely to see what the situation is. Do you need to replace something that has been lost? Is there less trust between you now? Do you need to work on returning to the patterns of love and respect that used to characterise your marriage?

You may find that the reality is not as bad as you expected. Maybe the vase is only chipped and not broken, after all. While you were angry, you may have exaggerated the strain that had been put on your marriage. Accepting the true situation means not looking for more ruin than is really there. Do not search for disaster, but, if it is present, do not close your eyes. Accept that this is the world in which you now live. Only then can you begin to make plans for improvement.

Once you have decided to let go of your fury with God, you begin to see how big an obstacle your fury was. When you were angry with God, you could not see him or feel him.

Then you could not pray or worship or read the Bible without turning aside in distaste. Now, having let go of your anger, you can see God again and you can begin to see the comfort that he offers you. You can begin to praise God again:

Praise the Lord.
Praise, O servants of the Lord,
praise the name of the Lord.
Let the name of the Lord be praised,
both now and for evermore.
From the rising of the sun to the place where it sets,
the name of the Lord is to be praised.
The Lord is exalted over all the nations,
his glory above the heavens.
Who is like the Lord our God,
the One who sits enthroned on high,
who stoops down to look
on the heavens and the earth?
He raises the poor from the dust
and lifts the needy from the ash heap;
he seats them with princes,
with the princes of their people.
He settles the barren woman in her home
as a happy mother of children.
Praise the Lord. (PSALM 113)

The reality is that our God is mighty and powerful. In the words of the psalmist, he even stoops to look on the heavens! He is high above everything (which gives him a good overview of complex situations). He can rearrange things as he pleases. Even those things that we call the 'laws' of nature and of physics do not constrain our God. He can do anything.

He can certainly provide anything that we need. He can bless us beyond anything we can imagine.

The reality is that God loves us, including all of us who cannot have children. He does not abandon us. This awesomely powerful being knows each one of us. He cares deeply about us and has a special concern for those who are in pain.

The reality is that God sees bigger pictures than we do. We may long for a baby, but God wants to set us in a happy home with a family. He may not go about building our home or our family in quite the way we expect, but what he has in mind is bigger and more satisfying that what we are working towards. We want one small thing for ourselves, but God plans on giving us the whole package.

The reality is that God transforms situations. He turns hopelessness into celebration. God can raise the poor from the dust and seat them with princes. He can turn circumstances around faster than any reality TV show. God can take an empty house and an empty heart and fill them with family and love. God can give you even more than you long to receive.

Father God, I am angry.
I know that anger can lead to sin and shame.
Please help me to get rid of my anger and blame.
Please help me to forgive those who have hurt me,
and to forgive myself for what I have done wrong.
I trust that you have a plan to help me grow closer to you
and more like you.
Please bless me with patience and peace. Amen

* CHAPTER 3 *

Hope and despair

'Every month I hope that this will be The Month.'

'Every time it doesn't happen, it feels like a new loss.'

'Each period feels like losing a baby.'

'Birthdays, anniversaries, any commemorative event, just remind me of how much time has passed. All I can think about is that yet another month has gone by, and I'm still not holding a baby!'

'Sometimes, something happens and I convince myself that it's a sign. I catch myself counting magpies and hoping that they're trying to tell me something! I will myself to feel sick in the mornings. I know all the signs of early pregnancy and I keep convincing myself that I've got them.'

'I can't stop taking pregnancy tests. Even when they're negative, I take another one the next day, hoping that I was just trying too soon! I find it so hard to accept that it hasn't happened, again!'

How to cope with hope

The distress of infertility is a cyclical distress. Every month I have another chance to conceive a child. Every month brings a new chance and a new failure. The repeated failure is much more distressing than one single failure would be. The fact that this time might be different, this month might be the miraculous blessed month in which a real baby is conceived, means that it is impossible to do away with hope altogether.

There are so many months of disappointment now that I do not know how to describe them. There have been so many days on which I have discovered that, once again, I am not going to have a baby. What should I say? Should I write about the days when I have lain on the floor and screamed into the carpet? Should I write about the times I have walked home from work with tears on my cheeks?

How can I write about the monthly cycle of hope, of trying, of desperate longing, of repeated, expected failure? Like a lot of infertile couples, my husband and I have a calendar on which we mark the days on which we make love and when my period starts. It is supposed to help us make love on the 'key days' when I am most likely to be ovulating. What it actually does is to provide a visual reminder of how many months pass in which we don't have a baby.

My family and friends have strongly recommended not getting my hopes up. That has not helped me at all. The truth is that my hope is already 'up'. I was brought up to believe that I would one day conceive a child. Most people who try to have a baby will succeed in having one. Not being an extraordinarily pessimistic person, I didn't expect to have any difficulty in conceiving a child.

The media, movies, novels, even the real-life experiences of friends, have led me to believe that it is easy to get pregnant. I have been warned many times about the danger of 'unwanted' or 'unplanned' pregnancies. I am aware of the huge range of products that are provided to help people avoid getting pregnant. All of this bellows the message, from many sides, that pregnancy is natural and easy to achieve. I could not help having high hopes when I began trying to conceive a child.

Some monthly cycles, I am distracted. Some days I am not thinking about whether or not I am pregnant. But the reality is that as long as I want to have a baby, I cannot stop myself hoping that I will one day do so. On those months when I have forgotten about it and my period comes as a surprise, I am not necessarily less upset than I am on months when I have thought of little else. The crushing disappointment is still crushing, whether I've been expecting it and anticipating it for days or it has suddenly hit me when I was thinking of something else. Because I have periods when I am not pregnant, I am rudely, crudely and messily reminded of my not-pregnant status every single month. I cannot forget it.

Hope is bound to occur, since what I desire is so natural, so normal, so common. People who hear about my trouble conceiving attempt to console me with stories of 'friends of friends' who tried for many years, were despaired of by doctors and then suddenly, miraculously conceived a perfect child. Such stories tease me with the idea that there is always hope. Miracle babies are conceived all the time.

So I find myself continuing to hope, even though every disappointing month dashes my hopes anew and sends me into a spiral of despair.

I do not think it is worth wasting any time in being angry with myself for hoping. That just means that I am burdened with guilt and frustration as well as the constant cycle of hope and despair.

The psalmist says:

Why are you downcast, O my soul?
Why so disturbed within me?
Put your hope in God,
for I will yet praise him,
my Saviour and my God.   (Psalm 42:11)

I might one day have a baby; it is not completely ridiculous to hope for such a day. But there are things about which I can be certain, and I should try to hope for them as well. I can trust that God has got a good plan for me, both in this world and in the world to come. I can hope that God will make me a better person. I can hope that I will live to see the good that he has prepared for me. I can hope that I will one day come face to face with a God who loves me.

When my hopes of conceiving a baby this month are dashed, I still have my hopes of being improved by God, being blessed by God, meeting with the loving God. Even though my hopes of having a child are destroyed and bring great despair, I am not left completely without hope. I hope that one day I will be able to praise God again. One day I will no longer despair about my infertility. It may be that the despair ends with the gift of a baby; it may be that it ends when the longing for a baby eases and passes away. God has a plan to ease despair and to replace it with praise; of that I am sure.

I cannot be sure that infertility is going to end in a healthy baby but I can be sure that I will have new reasons to praise God. Putting our hope in God doesn't mean believing that God is bound to give us anything and everything that we want. Putting our hope in God means believing that we will have reasons to praise God. When the psalmist addresses his soul, saying, 'Why are you downcast? ... I will yet praise

[God]', he could mean one of two things. He could mean that his soul need not be downcast because he will yet have reason to praise, or he could mean that he need not be downcast because he is going to choose to praise God. When he says, 'I will…' he might be predicting the future, being sure that soon he will praise God again, or he might be making a decision, declaring that he is going to praise God anyway.

We can all join the psalmist in this prophecy and declaration. We will have new reasons to praise God and we can choose to do so now, whatever we are currently feeling.

You, too, can be assured that God has a good plan for you. Whatever your future holds, it will hold new reasons for praising God. That is what it means to say that God is trustworthy and faithful. It means that God will continue to be himself. He will continue to be good and generous and loving. He will continue to give you good things and protect you from bad things. It doesn't mean that he will give you whatever you want and protect you from everything that you don't want (unfortunately), but he will nevertheless bring good into your life.

The psalmist takes control of his feelings, telling his soul that it shouldn't be downcast or disturbed; he is going to praise God. Choosing to praise God can actually make us feel better. It is what we are designed to do; it is our foremost purpose in life, and it feels good to do what we are made to do. We do not have to feel like praising God in order to do it. We do not have to be happy or even grateful in order to extol God. We can acknowledge his greatness and goodness, even if we feel miserable. We can choose to live our lives in praise and not in lamentation.

We can praise him now, even while our souls are downcast, because we praise God for who he is, not for what we are. We praise God because he is our Saviour and our God, the Creator and Redeemer of all. God is still God, even when we are feeling unhappy. We can rest secure that he will not change or fail.

Living despite hope

Having a baby is a life-changing experience, so many sensible people start to make room in their lives for a baby even as they start trying to conceive. You might have made decisions about where to live, where to work or how to spend your money, based on the understanding that you would soon have a child to consider. When that child doesn't arrive, you can easily find yourself trapped. I began writing this book in the living-room of my house because I had converted the second bedroom (which would have made a very fine home office) into a nursery. I have been unable to use one room of my house for over a year now, because it is the nursery.

Obviously, when I decorated and furnished my nursery, I assumed that it would not be empty for long. I thought I was sensibly decorating it in preparation, to save time and stress later when a baby arrived. Leaving the nursery decorated and waiting is an article of faith for me. If a child eventually comes, I want the child to know that I was waiting for him or her. But there may have to come a time when I dismantle the nursery and give away the furniture. I have discussed this with my husband and we have agreed that the room will remain as it is until a certain date. Then, if no child appears, we will transform the room into a study.

The important thing is to continue to live. Do not give up too much in preparation, or you will end up with nothing but an empty space. By all means devote one room of your house to your hope, but do not devote your entire house to your hope. You wanted a life that included a baby, not a baby instead of a life. Right now, you need to have a life that doesn't include a baby, not just an absence.

Reframing has meant reconsidering what my life looks like. I sat down to think about what I wanted my life to be and what it currently was. I wanted to assure myself that there was more to my life than not having any children. Here are the questions that I asked myself.

- How do you spend your time?
- What matters to you?
- What worries you?
- What do you enjoy?
- What are you good at?
- Whom do you love?
- Who loves you?

Then, considering setting myself new aims alongside that persistent aim of parenthood, I asked myself more questions.

- What would you like to do?
- What skills would you like to learn or improve?
- Whom would you like to see more often?
- What aspects of the world would you like to improve?

I wanted a full picture of my life today and what I would like it to be in the future. I wanted to find other targets and sources of hope, so that I could live a life of hope that doesn't revolve around hoping for a baby.

The final question on the second list may seem rather

ambitious, but a bit of ambition is a good thing. We are all capable of achieving a great deal and of making real changes in the world, perhaps giving others a reason to praise God in the process.

We all need to be hopeful about something. We all need to live for something. We all need a reason to be excited about the future. It cannot hurt to have a variety of hopes, lots of reasons to be excited about the future. None of us is a womb on legs. We all have other gifts to offer the world, other interests to explore and other plans to make. However much you long for a baby, there are always other things to long for as well.

Sometimes, waiting to have a baby can feel like being stuck in a perpetual Advent, never seeming to get any closer to Christmas Day. During Advent we talk about looking forward, but we are not looking forward to the birth of a baby. That happened a long time ago now. We need to live Advent lives, not hoping for the baby but hoping for the kingdom of God. We must look forward to life, not to birth.

Giving up hope

I have, as you might expect, been given a great deal of advice from a lot of people about how to cope with my infertility. I have been told by many people that I can have faith in God and trust that he is sure to give me a baby eventually, just as he did for Sarah and Hannah and Elizabeth. Unfortunately, God has not promised me a baby in the same way he promised one to Sarah, so I have no reason to expect that he will give me one. I have, of course, every right to expect God to keep promises that he has made to me, but I have no reason to expect him to keep promises that he has not made to me.

You may be in a different situation. You may feel you have received a definite promise from God. You may be certain that one day you will have the child for which you now long. If that is so, I can only suggest that you cling on to that promise and trust that it will be fulfilled.

In looking to the future, I found it helpful to draw up a long-term plan.

- Where will I live?
- What job will I do?
- What church will I attend?
- What church work will I do?
- Is there any other voluntary work I could do?
- Is there any other project I want to complete?

I thought about my answers to these questions for one year from now, five years from now, ten years from now, and 20 years from now.

I drew up several plans, looking at what might change if I had children. The real surprise for me was to see how little in my life really depended upon whether or not I had a baby. My marriage is the same, my skills are the same, and my interests are the same. Doubtless a baby would be life-changing, but it wouldn't be life-exchanging. Even my childless self can still get on with many of my other long-term plans. Even without having children, I can still begin to achieve some of the things that I want to achieve in life.

Any baby I have will grow up; he or she will not remain a baby for ever. So even if I do have a child, I will not be able to be caring for a tiny newborn baby for the rest of my life. Infertility has affected my ability to make long-term plans, but I realise that I cannot live for ever in limbo, always hoping that a baby will arrive and make everything fall into place.

Perhaps you are accustomed to playing the lottery. Perhaps you buy a ticket regularly or occasionally; you may enjoy spending a bit of time daydreaming about what would happen if you won—what you would buy with all that money. But would you consider giving up your job and simply sitting at home, waiting to win the lottery? Of course not! You cannot plan your life around winning the lottery, something over which you have no control. By all means play the lottery (if you conscience allows it), and, if you win, you will probably have to make a few adjustments. But the truth is that you need to have a plan for how you will live if you don't win the lottery.

Let's not lie awake wondering how we will cope if we win the lottery of having a baby. We can cross that bridge if and when we get to it. Let's plan how we're going to live if we don't win the lottery. Being prepared for a baby that never comes is as absurd as making no preparations for one that does. Infertile people must plan for a life even without a child. We still have a future.

Growing a new hope

'Hope deferred makes the heart sick, but a longing fulfilled is a tree of life' (Proverbs 13:12). When we hope for things but don't get them, it can lead us into a place so miserable that it can make us physically ill. When the months and months of waiting turned into years of unfulfilled longing, my body began to react. I began to feel tired all the time, and to get mild headaches and various other minor complaints. I lost weight and became listless.

As Proverbs tells us, hope that is never satisfied can lead to depression. Deferred hope can make you miserable, stressed and physically ill. If you are suffering from extreme stress or depression, you need to speak to your GP. Our minds, souls and bodies are connected in ways that are not yet fully understood. Prolonged unhappiness can cause serious problems, and these must be dealt with by a professional. If you notice any changes in your personality or physical fitness that you don't understand, do get help.

How well I know the despair that comes when hopes are dashed. Every negative pregnancy test leads to that horrible feeling. Every bit of bad news that you get dashes your hopes of a baby anew. You may already have reached the point of despair in your journey of infertility; you may indeed have been there many times by now.

All of us need fulfilled longings, not deferred hope. If we cannot change the future and ensure that we get what we were hoping for, perhaps it is time to change what we hope for. The old saying goes that we should never put all our eggs in one basket (if you drop the basket, you lose all your eggs at once). We should never put all of our hope in one possible future; we need to have other avenues for joy and triumph. We all need to want more than one thing in life: we need a hope that we can rely upon, a longing that we can be sure will be fulfilled.

There is a hope that will never be dashed. If you hope for God's promises to be fulfilled, you will never be disappointed. Paul tells us:

> We also rejoice in our sufferings, because we know that suffering produces perseverance; perseverance, character; and character, hope. And hope does not disappoint us, because God has poured out his love into our hearts by the Holy Spirit, whom he has given us.   (ROMANS 5:3–5)

Although Paul tells us to rejoice in sufferings, he does not tell us to seek them out. Don't deliberately make yourself feel worse! Don't avoid seeking help in order to gain more perseverance. At the same time, when we suffer, we can trust that some good will come out of our suffering. We may be strengthened by a time of testing.

It seems strange to read that 'suffering produces perseverance; perseverance, character; and character, hope'. I would have expected that suffering would teach a person to have a less hopeful personality, not a more hopeful one. I think, though, that it is about moving the focus of our hope. If we can learn to trust in God and not in ourselves, we will have a hope that will not be disappointed.

Suffering can teach us to trust in God rather than in ourselves. As we suffer, we experience our own failure. When people suffer, it is because they cannot take control of their own lives (if they were in control, of course, they would stop their own suffering), and learning to live with a lack of control can teach us to trust God.

As we realise that we cannot control the building of our family, we are able to relinquish control of this important area of our life to God; it can then be easier to accept that we cannot control other things. Learning to trust God's decision about when we will have a child can prepare us to trust his decisions about other aspects of our lives, too. Putting up with the loss of control in that area of life can make us calmer when we lose control over other areas. We can find the strength to keep going because we have learnt that life doesn't end simply because we cannot control it. Although a lack of control is frightening, it is not always life-threatening. Sometimes, events outside our control still turn out well.

Being able to keep going when we are thwarted makes us

stronger people. Relying on God to take care of whatever is beyond our control helps us to grow closer to him. As we relax about relinquishing control, we see more and more areas in which we have to trust him.

If a good friend said, 'Come over here; I've got something for you,' you would probably go willingly. You would certainly hope that they intended to give you something nice. If a complete stranger said the same thing, though, you would probably be rather wary. It takes time to build trust. The more often we go to God and see that he has good things to give us, the more trust we will have in him. The more often we offer our concerns to God in prayer, the more we will see that he can be trusted.

Even during this dark period when God has refused to answer my petition for a child, he has answered other prayers. He answered my prayers for my husband to find a new job. He answered my prayers for my mum's healing from cancer. He answered my prayers for a new and supportive church when I moved house. God has not deserted me. I have seen God answer these prayers, and I am convinced that he wants what is best for me. So, when I am at my best, I can trust that he is making the best choice for me in not giving me a baby, yet.

I remember one month when someone came running up to me after they had completed their daily Bible study and said, 'You're going to get pregnant. God has told me.' I was very hopeful that month but no pregnancy occurred. I suppose that it might still turn out to be true, but I suspect that it might have been wishful thinking on the other person's part rather than a real promise from God.

The problem with this kind of wishful thinking is that when the baby doesn't come, the disappointment is doubled. I am not only disappointed because I still don't have that much-longed-for baby; I am also disappointed because it seems as though God has broken his promise.

The reality is that God doesn't break his promises, *ever*. I am so eager to have a child that I put promises into God's mouth and convince myself that he has said I will have a baby. If I am a day late starting my period and my daily Bible notes are about the story of Hannah, I get excited and think that maybe it is a sign from God. Maybe I'm pregnant...

Although we cannot pick the promises that we want God to make to us, the good news is that there are promises that God has made for each one of us. We can all be certain that he will fulfil those promises. For example, Jesus said, 'I have come that they may have life, and have it to the full' (John 10:10b). It's not the same as being promised a baby, but God has promised that he has come so that we might have 'life'. We can trust that, in him, we have forgiveness of all our sins, and that we will live for ever with Christ after the end of our earthly lives. We can also trust that our earthly lives will contain joy and peace and worthwhile work. We can trust that we will live a full life, a life that is full of love. We will not always feel empty.

Those are promises that we can trust. If we hope for those things, our hopes will not be dashed and we will not be disappointed.

My father wrote a song, which I often use as a prayer:

We know we need Your Spirit,
We know we need its touch,
We ask for things that please us,
Sometimes we ask too much.

But you will give us what we need,
Of that we can be sure,
And you have got a plan for us,
To help us love you more.

I pray that you and I might come to trust in God's plan for us. I cannot be sure that his plan includes a healthy body or even a light spirit, but I can be sure that his plan includes wisdom and knowledge. We can be sure that if we seek God, we will find him—and, once we do find him, I expect that will be enough.

Father God, I am disappointed.
I have been hoping for a baby,
and my hopes keep being disappointed.
Please help me to trust you
and to trust in your plan for me.
Please help me to put my hope in you
and to hope for the right things.
I know that faith is a gift from you,
so please give me the faith I need to trust you. Amen

✻ CHAPTER 4 ✻

Jealousy

'I almost hate people who have children.'

'I've tried to be a good person and a good Christian. I'm faithful to my husband. I tried to start a family when I was young and healthy. I took all the right vitamins. I followed all the advice. Why can't I have a baby? I deserve a baby!'

'Sometimes it seems like everyone apart from me is pregnant!'

'I was out for dinner with some colleagues and one of them was heavily pregnant. She started boasting about how she'd got pregnant the first month they'd tried. Her husband was sat there grinning from ear to ear and joked that he was "super virile". I wanted to throw my salad at them.'

'It's not fair!!'

'A heart at peace gives life to the body, but envy rots the bones,' says Proverbs 14:30.

Esau was the older of twin boys. According to contemporary law, Esau was entitled to his father's blessing and to inherit his father's wealth. However, Esau's younger brother, Jacob, bought Esau's right to inherit from him. When Esau had been out hunting for several days and returned home hungry and tired, Jacob refused to give him anything to eat unless Esau gave him his birthright. Esau reasoned that he couldn't inherit his father's wealth anyway if he died of starvation, so he agreed. Then, as if that wasn't bad enough, when their father Isaac was old and blind, Jacob dressed up and pretended to be Esau and so tricked Isaac into giving him Esau's blessing.

After this act of deception, Jacob ran away because he was afraid that Esau would attack him. Years later, having got on to bad terms with his uncle, with whom he had been living, Jacob returned home with his wives, children and the wealth that he had gained. Jacob was afraid of meeting Esau again, in case his brother was still angry with him—but he obviously didn't know Esau very well:

> Jacob looked up and there was Esau, coming with his four hundred men; so he divided the children among Leah, Rachel and the two maidservants. He put the maidservants and their children in front, Leah and her children next, and Rachel and Joseph in the rear. He himself went on ahead and bowed down to the ground seven times as he approached his brother.
>
> But Esau ran to meet Jacob and embraced him; he threw his arms around his neck and kissed him. And they wept. Then Esau looked up and saw the women and children. 'Who are these with you?' he asked.
>
> Jacob answered, 'They are the children God has graciously given your servant.'
>
> Then the maidservants and their children approached and bowed down. Next, Leah and her children came and bowed down. Last of all came Joseph and Rachel, and they too bowed down.

Esau asked, 'What do you mean by all these droves I met?'

'To find favour in your eyes, my lord,' he said.

But Esau said, 'I already have plenty, my brother. Keep what you have for yourself.'   (Genesis 33:1–9)

Esau must have known a fair bit about jealousy. His brother tricked him out of his birthright and their father's blessing, but here, years later, he doesn't seem jealous. How did he avoid such feelings? Why did his anger and resentment fade with time rather than festering?

The key word is 'acceptance'. Esau accepts his brother back into his life, greeting him affectionately. He accepts his brother's heartfelt apology and his brother's gift—after some persuasion (vv. 10–11). Esau does a lot of accepting in this passage, but the first and most important acceptance was his acceptance of his own lot in life.

Admittedly, the story of Esau is a bit patchy. We see Esau grieving over his losses (Genesis 27:34–38), but then the narrator follows Jacob's experiences and we see nothing more of Esau for over 14 years. We can assume, however, that Esau has accepted his lot in life. When Jacob offers him flocks and herds, Esau doesn't take them saying, 'Well, it's the least that you owe me.' He refuses, saying, 'I already have plenty, my brother. Keep what you have for yourself.' He is not jealous of Jacob's success, because he is quite happy with his own level of success. It is because he is grateful for what he has that Esau is able to feel at peace with Jacob's having so much.

I think this has a lot to teach us. If we can be satisfied with what we have, we are less likely to be jealous of what others have. I must learn to accept my lot in life, just as Esau did. If I am to avoid jealousy, I need also to accept my brothers and sisters. I need to accept other people's fertility. Esau greets Jacob with a hug and calls him 'brother'. This scene is uncannily similar to the scene towards the end of the prodigal son parable (told in Luke 15:11–32). In the Genesis story, though, instead of the father, it's the elder brother who runs up and embraces the returning runaway. Far from complaining at the runaway's welcome, Esau is instigating it. He 'ran to meet Jacob and embraced him; he threw his arms around his neck and kissed him. And they wept' (Genesis 33:4).

OK, Esau had a lot of time to recover from his brother's betrayal, but he used those 14 years to get over the betrayal rather than dwelling on it. We all have this choice. When we experience pangs of jealousy, we might need time to deal with our feelings. Time is only useful, though, if we spend it accepting the situation. If we spend it in resentment, we will simply be dragged down further by envy.

When Esau hugs Jacob and calls him 'brother', he is accepting Jacob as an equal. It is very tempting to put up walls between ourselves and those of whom we are jealous, and that doesn't help matters. If we want to rejoice in other people's good fortune, we have to feel some affinity with them. It is easier to say, 'My brother, keep what you have for yourself' than to say, 'Let them keep what they have.' In order to be happy for other people, I must feel some kind of affection for them.

As well as his gift, Esau accepts Jacob's apology with grace—and, in this instance, that means accepting it in silence. Apologies are among the hardest things to say, so, when we are receiving an apology from someone else, we should remember that and try to ease the situation as much as possible. By accepting Jacob's apology, by accepting

Jacob and by accepting his own lot in life, Esau overcomes jealousy.

I have tried hard to follow the example of Esau in accepting his brother's good fortune. My mother was blessed to have five healthy children and, while my husband and I have failed to start a family of our own, my sister and her husband have been blessed with two lovely children. I have tried to remember Esau and to embrace my family with joy, not jealousy.

Other people will have babies, even though I don't. That is a part of life. Even some people who do not particularly want to have children will have them, while my longing goes unfulfilled. I admit that, at times, I have felt extraordinarily jealous of other people and their easily won families. My jealousy has sprung up particularly when I have seen others who (it seems to me) mistreat their children. When I see people who do not cherish their children in the way that I would cherish mine, I become consumed with jealousy. It doesn't seem fair that they should have children when I don't.

I had pulled up outside my home, waiting to park the car in the drive, and I saw a woman pushing a pram with a toddler walking next to her. She was smoking a cigarette and yelling at her toddler. As I watched, she shoved her toddler very hard into a hedge. The toddler screamed. She grabbed his arm and dragged him along beside her. When I got home, I started crying. How come she had two children and I didn't have any? She wasn't even nice to them!

Of course, the problem was not with that woman. I have no idea what kind of day she'd been having before I witnessed her pushing her child. I don't know how irritating that child had been (although I do know enough about children to realise that toddlers have a surprisingly large capacity for irritating behaviour). I don't know if the child was genuinely hurt or just making a fuss. I don't really know what I saw happening in front of me; what I do know is what was happening inside me: I was intensely jealous of this woman and I was angry because a part of me thought that I deserved children more than she did. That kind of feeling was both perfectly understandable and completely unacceptable. If I indulge that sort of feeling, I will end up bitter, judgmental and distant from God.

Jealousy is a dangerous emotion, but it is a common problem for people and probably always has been. Jesus told a parable about jealousy, which we will look at now because I think that he puts into this story a technique for avoiding jealousy that we can easily apply to our own lives.

For the kingdom of heaven is like a landowner who went out early in the morning to hire men to work in his vineyard. He agreed to pay them a denarius for the day and sent them into his vineyard.

About the third hour he went out and saw others standing in the marketplace doing nothing. He told them, 'You also go and work in my vineyard, and I will pay you whatever is right.' So they went.

He went out again about the sixth hour and the ninth hour and did the same thing. About the eleventh hour he went out and found still others standing around. He asked them, 'Why have you been standing here all day long doing nothing?'

'Because no one has hired us,' they answered. He said to them, 'You also go and work in my vineyard.'

When evening came, the owner of the vineyard said to

his foreman, 'Call the workers and pay them their wages, beginning with the last ones hired and going on to the first.'

The workers who were hired about the eleventh hour came and each received a denarius. So when those came who were hired first, they expected to receive more. But each one of them also received a denarius. When they received it, they began to grumble against the landowner. 'These men who were hired last worked only one hour,' they said, 'and you have made them equal to us who have borne the burden of the work and the heat of the day.'

But he answered one of them, 'Friend, I am not being unfair to you. Didn't you agree to work for a denarius? Take your pay and go. I want to give the man who was hired last the same as I gave you. Don't I have the right to do what I want with my own money? Or are you envious because I am generous?' (MATTHEW 20:1–15)

Jealousy is caused by focusing too much on other people. We get jealous when we obsess about what others have got, rather than reflecting on what we've got in our own lives. I cannot actually arrange it so that nobody else gets the joy of a baby until we do (of course, I wouldn't really want that, even if I could do it). But I can try not to spend much time dwelling on thoughts of all the many people who do have children while I don't.

It all starts with disappointment. In the parable of the workers in the vineyard, the first group of workers expected to get more because they had been working for longer. When they weren't rewarded for their long service, they felt disappointed. In the same way, I feel disappointed when I don't get pregnant, when I don't find it as easy or as natural as I thought it would be to conceive a child.

In the passage, the first workers let their disappointment fester. They thought about what the other workers had. They thought about how easy it had been for the latecomers to earn their money and they contrasted that ease with their own difficulty in earning the same amount. Then they felt jealous and complained to the landowner that he had made the latecomers equal to them. For us, it has been a struggle to start a family, including embarrassment and effort and unpleasant side-effects. For a lot of people it is easy: it just happens. Sometimes I feel, like the jealous workers, that it is unfair that I should have to work so hard to get something that comes so easily to others.

Then comes resentment. The full-time workers complained that they had done the hardest work in the burning heat of midday. I complain that it isn't fair, it isn't right, I shouldn't have it harder than other people. How easy it is to start with disappointment on the fringe of jealousy, and then, by indulging in jealousy, to move into resentment.

Disappointment is a natural part of life, but resentment is far more deep-seated, so it is potentially far more dangerous than disappointment. Resentment is about holding grudges, about wanting other people to suffer at the same time as you. The initial workers were, at first, quite happy with their job but, once they became jealous of the latecomers, they started complaining about the hardness of the work and the heat of the day. Resentment leaves a bitter taste in the mouth, and it stops anything from tasting sweet. Watch out, or it will suck the joy out of life!

When the long-term labourers indulged their jealousy of the latecomers by moaning, they stopped being pleased with what they had already earned. They had made a deal with the landowner, and the landowner had kept the deal, but they couldn't see the justice in it. Their view of the world was corrupted by jealousy and they were no longer able to see that they had, in reality, been treated perfectly fairly. They started comparing themselves with the latecomers, just as I started comparing myself with the woman who had the two children. Without knowing anything about the landowner's deal with the latecomers, the first workers decided that they were more deserving and should have been more substantially rewarded. This is comparable with my behaviour when I witnessed the woman pushing her child. Without knowing anything about her or anything about how I would really deal with her circumstances, I made a judgment. I decided that I was more deserving of a child, and I felt angry and jealous.

The landowner says, 'Friend, I am not being unfair to you. Didn't you agree to work for a denarius? Take your pay and go' (vv. 13–14). In other words, accept the deal that you made; accept what you've got. The landowner tells his jealous workers that they need to stop staring at others and focus on their own relationship with him. The words of that landowner are God's words to those of us who are jealous today: 'Friend, I am not being unfair to you. Haven't I given you everything that I promised to give you?'

One of the worst things about jealousy is that it stops us enjoying the things that we have. But it also works the other way around: if we remember to enjoy what we have, that can stop us from being jealous. As Paul says, 'Give thanks in all circumstances' (1 Thessalonians 5:18). We should stop looking at other people's good fortune and blessings and look instead at our own good fortune and blessings. If we are jealous, that jealousy can destroy thankfulness; but, if we are thankful, that thankfulness can destroy jealousy.

When I look at other people with their children, I am still

tempted to feel jealous, but now I know how to escape the trap of jealousy. If I can turn my eyes away from others and towards God, I can count my blessings. If I can think of what God has given me rather than worrying about what God has given others, I can enjoy what I have without envying those who have different lives and different gifts from mine.

Father God, I am jealous.
Other people have things that I want
and it makes me unhappy.
I know that you have given me many blessings.
Please help me to be grateful for what I've got
and not to envy others.
Thank you for loving me
and for sending your only Son to die for me.
Thank you for being with me and for bearing with me,
even when I'm moody. Amen

Confusion and decision-making

'I don't know what to do!'

'I had a nightmare that I was sitting in a consultant's office and they were trying to rush me into a room and start injecting me with drugs. They wouldn't let me discuss it, or even give me any time to think about it.'

'It feels like we've started this whole process rolling and the doctors assume that we're going to move from one step to another. I'm just not sure if this is the route that I want to take.'

'I can't imagine not having a baby. I don't want to think about anything else. My husband thinks it's time to talk about adoption, but I can't bear to give up on my own baby.'

'IVF seems like a huge step to take. I don't know if I could cope if it failed.'

'Would the baby still be mine, if I used a donor or a surrogate? How do I know if I'd regret it?'

'Nobody will tell me what to do next! They keep presenting me with "options" and I just don't know which ones to choose.'

'I'm too fragile to make big decisions.'

Guide me, O Thou great Redeemer,
Pilgrim through this barren land.
I am weak, but Thou art mighty;
Hold me with Thy powerful hand.
Bread of Heaven,
Feed me now and ever more.
WILLIAM WILLIAMS (1745)

Becoming a patient

There are three stages of infertility.

- Trying for a baby.
- Becoming a patient and undergoing fertility treatments.
- Giving up trying for a baby.

Moving from one stage to another is a big step, fraught with worries and stress. Moving from one stage to another can feel like an admission of failure. It sometimes feels easier to delay the move. When you're trying for a baby, it can seem like a drastic step to seek the help of a doctor; giving up on treatment and moving on can feel like admitting defeat.

The first time I visited a doctor to ask for help, I took on a new identity. I became a patient; I was suddenly officially 'infertile'. Moving from being just a normal couple who wanted a baby to a couple who were infertile was a big step, and it brought home once again quite how important it was to me.

It was not, however, the last big step that I had to take. Dealing with infertility raises big questions and requires difficult decisions to be made. However, I believe that God is willing to help me make the right decisions, even if the process is a hard one.

Be merciful to me, O Lord, for I am in distress;
my eyes grow weak with sorrow,
my soul and my body with grief.
My life is consumed by anguish
and my years by groaning;
my strength fails because of my affliction,
and my bones grow weak.   (PSALM 31:9–10)

Infertility is a serious health issue. One of the results of any chronic illness is a lack of trust in your own body. Once your body has failed you in an important way, it can be hard to trust it again. Barrenness can come to define you and your body, but this is not a healthy way to live. Your body belongs to you and you need to take care of it, because the experiences of your body will affect your mind and your soul as well.

God created our bodies and he loves them. God created my body and he thinks that it is beautiful. Even when I am not pleased with the sight of my body, God is pleased with it because God doesn't do shoddy work. It doesn't matter whether I really feel that to be true; it remains true whether I feel it or not.

When Christ came to earth as a man, he came in a normal human body. He did not come as an angel or as a superman. His normal body got tired and hungry and ultimately died, and in this way Christ sanctified the human body. This is a wonderful mystery of our faith.

I must remember that the main task of my body has never been to make a baby; my body was made to honour God. It is with our hands that we do God's work and it is with our feet that we go where God sends us. Our bodies are our instruments of service for God. Whatever failings my body may have, it is still useful and important for praising God, for spreading the good news and for doing God's work.

Paul writes, 'Do you not know that your body is a temple of the Holy Spirit, who is in you, whom you have received from God? You are not your own; you were bought at a price. Therefore honour God with your body' (1 Corinthians 6:19–20).

When we become a Christian, we are baptised. In the moment of baptism (whether it happens when we are infants or adults), we involve our entire bodies in a ceremony of commitment to God. We are not expected to keep our belief and our commitment inside our heads; we are expected to involve our whole body in the act of committing ourselves to Christ. In baptism it is not only our souls that are cleansed of the sins that we have committed; it is also our bodies. They are made clean and holy and set aside for God's service.

In the sacrament of Communion, we take the body and blood of Christ into our own bodies by eating the bread and the wine. Just as baptism cleanses the body from the outside, so Communion cleanses the body from the inside. I am not saying that baptism or Communion are solely matters of the body, but they do have to involve the body. Your body is not a mere vessel that you will set aside when you die. Your body is an integral part of yourself and of your faith. Your body is as committed to God and as connected to Christ as your soul is. Our faith does not give us the option of ignoring our bodies. Instead, it urges us to love and to honour our bodies.

As an infertile woman, I have been deeply ashamed of my body. I have been ashamed of my womb that cannot carry a baby to term and of my breasts that will not feed a baby milk. I have considered all of the parts that make me a woman to be dishonourable and unpresentable because they are dysfunctional.

Reading Paul's words in 1 Corinthians 6 helped me to see how far away from a healthy body image I had allowed myself to get. I ought to be protecting and honouring the weaker parts of my body, not despising and rejecting them. In rejecting my own body, I mentally dissociated myself from it. I took less and less interest in dressing myself attractively or taking care of myself. I was angry with the curves that made me look womanly and I dressed in looser clothing in order to conceal them. I felt that having womanly hips and large breasts was a sort of physical lie, because I looked like a fertile woman but I wasn't one.

I don't need to think that I'm the best-looking woman in the world to have a healthy body image. Having a healthy body image means accepting your body as it is and understanding that it is an integral part of your self. Having a healthy body image means caring for your body and recognising how your body feels and what it needs. Caring for your body is about feeding your body the foods that it needs (not only the tastes that your mouth craves) and giving it the exercise that it requires.

It doesn't need to take a lot of effort to enjoy your body. Any pleasurable physical experience can help. I have never run a marathon; nor do I spend a lot of time trying on clothes or doing my make-up. Going for a walk, swimming, sunbathing, having a warm shower—all these activities have helped me to experience my body as a positive and beautiful part of who I am. It has been important for me to take some time to appreciate and care for my body, and to remember that I am not defined by infertility.

Staying together

Of course it is necessary for your doctor to examine you and your partner separately. It may also be necessary for your doctor to treat one of you and not the other. The rationale for this action does not mean that it is any easier to handle. Making a baby is almost certainly something that you thought of as a joint task. You probably thought of your potential child as someone who would spring from your loving marriage. When we married, my husband and I became 'one flesh', so it was very hard to divide that flesh up again in order to work out what was going wrong.

When we decided to talk to a doctor about our trouble conceiving, we decided that, whatever the news was, we would keep it between ourselves. I wanted to model our re-action on the last few lines of the play *Who's Afraid of Virginia Woolf?*

In the play, George and Martha have been playing host to Nick and Honey. Nick finds out that George and Martha were never able to have children.

Nick [to George; quietly]: You couldn't have... any?
George: We couldn't.
Martha [a hint of communion in this]: We couldn't.[2]

Even though I couldn't ensure that our infertility was equally shared between my husband and me, I wanted to give the impression to everyone outside our marriage that it was equally shared. I wanted that 'hint of communion' between us. It is possible to persist in viewing your infertility as something that belongs to both of you, and I think that it helps.

Paul writes, 'Husbands ought to love their wives as their own bodies. He who loves his wife loves himself. After all, no one ever hated his own body, but he feeds and cares for it, just as Christ does the church—for we are members of his body' (Ephesians 5:28–30).

You can love your partner's body as if it were your body; your partner can love your body as if it were their body. Even if the infertility resides in the body of only one of you, that body belongs to both of you. You can share the sorrow and the grief; you can make sure that the infertility belongs to both of you equally. When making medical decisions, it matters whose body is having trouble, but, when dealing with emotions, it makes no difference whatsoever.

I found it really helpful to have my husband with me during medical procedures. We are separate people. If one member of a couple is undergoing treatment or has received a diagnosis, and the other hasn't, it is ridiculous to pretend that both partners are enduring the same experience. We can only do our best to stand side by side, because there are necessary limits to our unity and these should not be sources of guilt. We can love each other's bodies 'as' our bodies, but they cannot actually be our bodies. We cannot undergo one another's pain and we cannot deal with one another's infertility.

If your partner has a diagnosis and you haven't, they will be undergoing a different experience from yours. You cannot really understand what they're going through; you can only offer support. I think that is why the three lines from *Who's Afraid of Virginia Woolf?* appealed to me. They only suggest 'a hint of communion', and that was something that we could achieve, even if we couldn't exactly split the burden between us.

Making choices

Fertility treatment is moving fast. People who do not need to consult a fertility expert for any reason may never have given any thought to the morality of such treatments. It was very important to my husband and myself, however, that we didn't commit to a course of action that we would later regret.

For us, this meant considering the downside of various treatments as well as the possible triumphant end result. We found ourselves discussing at what point life begins, what cellular bodies we felt comfortable about destroying, and how important we think genetic heritage is to a child and an adult. We discussed how we might explain a child's beginning to them and how much information we wanted to share with friends and family. It was very important to us to consider all these issues before we took any particular course of fertility treatment.

It may sound awful to ask about what is destroyed in the course of fertility treatment, but we didn't want to add regret to all the other emotions we were experiencing. We believed it would be easier to reconcile ourselves to what we were going to do before we did it.

Just because I want to have a baby, it does not mean that I am bound to take any route that is offered. There's no competition for the most desperate-to-become-a-parent. There are no prizes for being willing to undergo absolutely anything in the quest for a baby.

I have not mentioned here what our discussions were or what decisions we made, because I don't think that would be helpful. It is impossible to tell anyone what you have chosen to do in this situation without implying that you are judging them for taking a different course of action. These decisions are hard and, ultimately, we must make them for ourselves. I do think, however, that God helped to guide my husband and me in our decision and that he will guide anyone who asks him.

What is right?

It is not very popular these days even to suggest that there are rights and wrongs to do with fertility treatment. There are some extreme views out there, and some people will judge your decisions very harshly indeed if you disagree with their own. However sensitive the issue is, we cannot ignore it.

Once we have given our lives over to God, we belong to him. There is no aspect of our lives that we can withhold from God. If we will not acknowledge him as Lord of all our being, we may as well reject him totally. God will not share us; he wants to rule every aspect of our lives.

We would not try to take one day off from our faith every week. We cannot be a Christian on every day except Wednesday, for example! Once we have decided to follow Christ, we follow him every day of the week. We would not understand a person who said that they would follow Christ's rules everywhere except on a boat. That would be ridiculous! Every time they wanted to do something that they knew God would forbid, they would simply board their boat and get on with going their own way. We would consider such a person two-faced, silly and dangerously misled; we would not accept what they were doing as a sensible way to live.

Nor can we be a Christian in everything except our sex lives. God belongs in the bedroom just as much as he does in every other room in the house, so we do not consider that we can do absolutely anything we want with our bodies. When having sex, just as when we do anything else, we must remember to love our neighbour and to worship our God. If we are people of faith, we cannot ignore our faith when we make decisions about that area of life.

Unless the Lord builds the house,
its builders labour in vain.
Unless the Lord watches over the city,
the watchmen stand guard in vain.
In vain you rise early
and stay up late,
toiling for food to eat—
for he grants sleep to those he loves.
Sons are a heritage from the Lord,
children a reward from him.   (PSALM 127:1–3)

We probably did not wish to make the journey of infertility on our own. We may have longed to journey beside God, following the path that he laid out for us. I wanted to do the right thing at every stage of my journey through the barren land, but I have not found it at all easy to decide what is the right thing for my husband and me.

There are, of course, three main ways of determining the will of God:

- Reading the Bible.
- Listening to what other Christians have to say.
- Praying and heeding the promptings of the Holy Spirit.

Of course, it is still possible to make mistakes. If you try all three methods and still fail to reach peace of mind regarding major life decisions, you will merely be the latest in a very long line of respectable Christians who have done just the same thing. However, I do believe that God answers our prayers for guidance, and I believe that he will make an effort to communicate his will to you. God wants you to follow him, so he wants you to know how to do so. He will not leave you abandoned and without guidance.

I found Robert Winston's book *A Child Against All Odds* very helpful. As a Jewish man, he has drawn heavily on Old Testament teaching and stories in his consideration of the moral aspects of assisted fertility. As Winston is also a fertility specialist, he is able to go into detail about a variety of treatments.

I would only like to point out that what is right is intertwined with what is possible and what you feel most comfortable doing. Part of loving our neighbour is loving our partner, so it cannot be right to force our partner to do something that they really don't want to do. Another part of loving our neighbour is respecting the laws under which we live, so it cannot be right to do something illegal or, at best, legally dubious. God doesn't ask us to do the impossible, so what is possible for us may be one way of discerning God's guiding hand.

My mother has a saying: 'Just because something is unpleasant, it doesn't mean that God wants you to do it.' We can get trapped into thinking that God wants us to be unhappy and that following the 'narrow path' (see Matthew 7:13–14) has to be difficult. Certainly, it is sometimes very hard to follow the will of God, but we can trust that God likes us and wants us to be happy, safe and fulfilled.

There's a wonderful story in 2 Kings 4:1–7, where a widow has so little money that she is about to sell herself and her sons into slavery. All she has left is a tiny bit of oil. She goes to the prophet Elisha and he tells her to collect jars and fill them with oil. She does this and, lo and behold, her oil miraculously keeps flowing. It doesn't run out until she has filled every one of the jars she's collected. She then runs back to Elisha and tells him what has happened. He tells her to go home, sell the oil and use the money to pay off her debts and feed her family. I think it's wonderful that the widow didn't grasp at the miraculous oil and do what she thought was best: she went back to God's spokesman and asked him what to do with it.

A lot of us are afraid to run to God and ask him what to do with our 'jars of oil'. We're afraid that, if we offer what we have to God, he will say something that amounts to 'Sell it all, give the money to the poor and let yourself and your sons be sold into slavery.' We don't trust that sometimes God will say, 'Take care of yourself and your family.' But that is what God does. He likes us and he doesn't go out of his way to make us miserable. We can come to God and seek his will and we can be sure that the result will be for our good. It is difficult to discern God's will, but it is a safe thing for us to do.

Moving forward

Whatever fertility treatments you choose, they may not ultimately be successful. For my husband and me, they were not successful. The story of infertility does not have to stop there, however. There are several ways of moving forward from fertility treatment. Although I have not chosen to write about the conclusions that we eventually reached, I feel it might be helpful if I share some of my thoughts on a number of possible options.

Being child-free

Paul quotes the prophet Isaiah: 'Be glad, O barren woman, who bears no children; break forth and cry aloud, you who have no labour pains; because more are the children of the desolate woman than of her who has a husband' (Galatians 4:27; Isaiah 54:1). God turns the world upside down. He frees the prisoners; he gives sight to the blind; he raises the dead. He gives children to the barren woman.

Whatsoever your future holds, you can be sure that God will bless you. God takes special care of those who have suffered, so we can be sure that, whether in this world or the next, you will be blessed. So it is that God tells you, even in your barrenness, to be glad.

If you are infertile, you already know quite a lot about being child-free, since that is what you may have been for your entire adult life. Until it is a deliberate choice, however, it can be hard to focus on the positive aspects. If you are considering remaining child-free, try to think about what you will gain as well as what you will lose. Being free of children gives you space to fill with other commitments. It stops you being tied to schools and school schedules. Remaining childless may mean that you and your partner can both concentrate on your careers or your hobbies or your voluntary work, all without having to seek out childcare. If you do not have to make your home child-friendly, you might find that you can make it guest-friendly, thus opening up new opportunities for using your gift of hospitality.

Choosing to remain child-free is different from remaining unable to have children. It puts you back in control of the situation. Even if you have found infertility very difficult and distressing, you may find that being child-free is liberating rather than empty. Making that choice redefines infertility and stops it from being an issue in your life. It no longer matters whether or not you could have a child, if you have decided not to have one.

Environmental issues and worries about future global population growth may help you to view your choice in a wider context, as a service to the world in general and not merely a solution to your own problem of infertility. There are few who would argue that our planet needs a lot more people to be born into it. Deciding that you will be one of the people who forgoes the joy of a baby, saving the planet from one more mouth and one more polluter, could be one of the ways in which you preserve God's planet as it is.

Choosing to remain child-free may be a difficult decision. You will have to let go of your quest for a baby. You may also have to face some criticism from friends and family. When you choose to remain child-free, you are also choosing not to give your parents grandchildren. Depending on your current relationship with your parents, this may be of little or of great consequence to them and to you. If you find that your usual support network has difficulty supporting you in this choice, you may find it helpful to seek out others who have made the same choice (see the organisations list at the end of this book for some ideas).

According to our faith, you will not, in fact, be without children because of your childlessness. This doesn't mean that everyone who remains child-free has to work with children. You might be a godparent or a Sunday school teacher, but you certainly don't have to be. What it does mean is that all the people you help in this world are, in a sense, your children. To bring up children is to guide, to lead, to set an example, to protect and to provide. These are all things that you can still do, and, if you do them, you will have children enough. You will have an impact on the world and make it a better place. You will leave a legacy behind you. You will bear fruit.

There is a character in C.S. Lewis's book *The Great Divorce*, called Sarah Smith, who had no children on earth but is surrounded by a great crowd of them in heaven. The narrator and his guide converse:

'And who are all these young men and women on each side?'

'They are her sons and daughters.'

'She must have had a very large family, Sir.'

'Every young man or boy that met her became her son— even if it was only the boy that brought the meat to her back door. Every girl that met her was her daughter.'

'Isn't that a bit hard on their own parents?'

'No. There *are* those that steal other people's children. But her motherhood was of a different kind. Those on whom it fell went back to their natural parents loving them more. Few men looked on her without becoming, in a certain fashion, her lovers. But it was the kind of love that made them not less true, but truer, to their own wives.' [3]

Sarah Smith's love and care for others gives her more children than she could possibly have had on earth. This wonderful scene reminds us that it is not necessary to have children in order to love them. It is not only parents who love others, care for others, lead others and leave an impression on those whom they meet. All the love that you may once have thought of sharing with your children can be very profitably shared with those who are not your biological children. We too can have a 'motherhood of a different kind'.

If you make the decision to remain childless on earth, you can still be an important guide and mentor. You can still be a protector, a nurturer, a provider. The gifts that you dreamt of giving to your own children need not go to waste. You can still be important to the next generation.

There is joy for the childless. This may be hard for you to imagine in the midst of your quest for a child, but children are not the only source of joy in anyone's life. They are not even the most important source of joy. True joy, full joy, comes from God alone. If you finally decide or finally realise that it is best for you to live without children, you can trust that God still has a plan for you. There are other important ways of bearing fruit, other tasks on this earth, other relationships. Without children, you will still be you, and God has promised to be with you.

Adopting

You may decide that you should build your family by parenting a child who isn't genetically yours. If you do choose to adopt, or feel called to adopt (it is as much of a vocation as a calling to the ministry or missionary work), you can find help from many books about adoption, to do with the specific planning and decision-making involved.

Adoption is something that many infertile people choose to do and feel called to do. It is not, however, a cure for infertility; it is a way to live as an infertile person.

> 'Though you were ruined and made desolate
> and your land laid waste,
> now you will be too small for your people,
> and those who devoured you will be far away.
> The children born during your bereavement

will yet say in your hearing,
"This place is too small for us;
give us more space to live in."
Then you will say in your heart,
"Who bore me these?
I was bereaved and barren;
I was exiled and rejected.
Who brought these up?
I was left all alone,
but these—where have they come from?"'
This is what the Sovereign Lord says:
'See, I will beckon to the Gentiles,
I will lift up my banner to the peoples;
they will bring your sons in their arms
and carry your daughters on their shoulders.
Kings will be your foster fathers,
and their queens your nursing mothers.
They will bow down before you with their faces to the
ground;
they will lick the dust at your feet.
Then you will know that I am the Lord;
those who hope in me will not be disappointed.'

(Isaiah 49:19–23)

This passage from Isaiah brings up some of the pain and struggle that are integral to adoption. The story of adoption begins with desolation and grief. Children enter adoptive homes because they have left their first homes. This is always a sad experience and is frequently a cause of lasting emotional and mental scars. You can read more about the different sides of adoption in *The Adoption Experience* by Ann Morris.

Ultimately, Isaiah's view of adoption is wonderfully positive. Adoption is one way in which suffering can be transformed into joy and emptiness can be filled. The children who have been failed by their first parents can be helped by their forever family. The parents who were missing a child to love can find one. The parents who were unable to give their children the love and support that is necessary can be sure that their children will get that love and support elsewhere.

Adoption is another long and sometimes painful journey. You may find that there are difficulties and disappointments involved in your attempt to adopt children. Although the pain of infertility will probably never disappear for good, the process of adoption can bring new pains and sorrows. When you decide to adopt, you are beginning another story, which may bring your happy ending—but it will be the ending of your adoption journey, not of your infertility.

Fostering

Fostering has many similarities to adoption. It is also about uniting two families and two different pasts. It also requires a great deal of courage and determination and begins with a stressful assessment process.

Whatever family arrangements you find your household containing, you can be sure that God will be with you. He will understand what you are going through and he will support you in your important work.

Luke tells an enlightening story about Jesus' childhood:

Every year his parents went to Jerusalem for the Feast of the Passover. When he was twelve years old, they went up to the Feast, according to the custom. After the Feast was over, while his parents were returning home, the boy Jesus stayed behind in Jerusalem, but they were unaware of it.

Thinking he was in their company, they travelled on for a day. Then they began looking for him among their relatives and friends. When they did not find him, they went back to Jerusalem to look for him. After three days they found him in the temple courts, sitting among the teachers, listening to them and asking them questions. Everyone who heard him was amazed at his understanding and his answers. When his parents saw him, they were astonished. His mother said to him, 'Son, why have you treated us like this? Your father and I have been anxiously searching for you.'

'Why were you searching for me?' he asked. 'Didn't you know I had to be in my Father's house?' But they did not understand what he was saying to them.

Then he went down to Nazareth with them and was obedient to them. But his mother treasured all these things in her heart. And Jesus grew in wisdom and stature, and in favour with God and men. (LUKE 2:41–52)

Jesus had a complicated family relationship, too. He was fostered by his earthly father, Joseph, but his loyalty to his heavenly Father remained strong throughout his life. The short story that we see in Luke contains the only information that we have about Jesus' childhood. Whatever complicated family relationships you build, God has been there before you and he knows the emotional turmoil that you are going through.

Whether it is early or late in your infertility journey, whether you are hopeful or despairing, whether you are alone or surrounded by supportive family and friends, God is with you. God has been with you throughout your past. He is within you now, intimate in his knowledge of your feelings and thoughts. He is ahead of you, preparing the way and beckoning you onwards.

Father God, I am not perfect,
but you made me and all your work is good.
You are pleased with me.
Please help me to see the beauty of your creation in myself.
Please help me to enjoy what I can do
and not to worry so much about what I can't do.
I know that my body is your creation and your temple.
I pray that your Holy Spirit would will inside me
and fill the empty spaces. Amen

Disappointment and letting go

'It wasn't meant to be this hard.'

'I had this image of what our children would look like. I had a plan of the perfect age gaps. I never imagined that it wouldn't happen the way I planned it.'

'I thought that it was up to me to decide when I wanted children and how many I wanted. Now it seems as though I have no say in this at all.'

'Not being able to give my husband a son. That's the worst part.'

'I have a drawer full of gorgeous baby clothes. I just need the baby to put in them.'

'When we were dating, my now-husband once sent me a postcard with a picture of three children holding hands and running down the beach. He wrote a caption on the postcard saying that this was what he imagined our children would be like. That picture is branded on my mind. Where are those children?'

Most of us have a picture of ourself, a picture of our marriage and a picture of our future. We can see what they *ought* to look like. Sometimes, when things are going well and we are not disappointing ourselves, we can believe that things really are as we would like them to be. Often we can—or, at least, we think we can—fool others into believing that the perfect fiction is real. Infertility is one of those untidy things that ruins the perfect fiction, however. We cannot hide it from ourselves or from others. It is obvious that we are not perfect, our marriage is not perfect, and our future will not be perfect.

Part of dealing with my infertility has been to accept that I am not the perfect person I wanted to be. I have found that mourning the loss of my imagined 'perfect' life has helped to open me up to enjoy the life I actually have.

Letting go of the perfect you

> Then God said, 'Let us make man in our image, in our likeness, and let them rule over the fish of the sea and the birds of the air, over the livestock, over all the earth, and over all the creatures that move along the ground.'
>
> So God created man in his own image, in the image of God he created him; male and female he created them.
>
> God blessed them and said to them, 'Be fruitful and increase in number; fill the earth and subdue it. Rule over the fish of the sea and the birds of the air and over every living creature that moves on the ground.' (GENESIS 1:26–28)

Fertility is the natural state of all creatures. A gene-centred view of history tells us that the sole purpose of life is to replicate itself. Richard Dawkins, for example, writes in the first chapter of *River out of Eden*, 'Each generation is a filter, a sieve: good genes tend to fall through the sieve to the next generation; bad genes tend to end up in bodies that die young or without reproducing.'[4] All of this can easily lead people who are dealing with infertility to think of themselves as unnatural and useless. It is not particularly flattering to think of yourself as the repository of genes too 'bad' to be passed on to the next generation.

The first commandment that God gave to humans was to 'be fruitful'. The pressure to be fruitful is a very real pressure, both socially and religiously. The assumption that those who do not have children are somehow selfish is a prevailing one. Barrenness used to be seen as a curse by most early societies and it is not easy to escape the relics of that viewpoint. Infertility has made me feel unnatural, cursed and useless.

It may be helpful to remember, though, that infertility is not at all unnatural. In fact, it has been around for a very long time. Plenty of animals and people have experienced infertility before you or I. It really is a part of the world in which we live.

It may also help if you try to get a wider perspective on life. There are probably other things that you cannot do. I can't play a single musical instrument, I can't speak foreign languages, I can't draw, and I'm quite short. None of these disadvantages has ever upset me in the same way that infertility has done. There are occasions on which I would like to be different from the person I am, but most of the time I accept the limits of my capabilities. Infertility is really just one small thing that limits me, just like any of the other small things that limit me.

To take another angle on the same idea, remind yourself of the things that you can do. I am quite a good cook, I can put together an interesting Sunday school lesson, and I know my way around computers. I am sure there are plenty of things that you do well. Some of them may have taken a lot of practice; some may require a great deal of effort. When you get down to it, being good at something that takes a long time to learn or something that requires a great deal of skill or concentration is much more impressive that simply being born able to conceive and bear children! Your skills and your talents tell the world what you are really like. You are not characterised by your infertility.

Infertility is an invisible illness. Although the absence of children in your family may seem very obvious and noticeable to you, it is probably not as glaring to other people as you might think. If you consider the qualities you admire most in your friends, I doubt that fertility ranks very highly. If you are not impressed by other people's ability to have children, you can safely assume that they are not scornful of your inability to do the same.

You are not perfect. That shouldn't really come as a shock. What is shocking is that God has a plan to make you (and me) perfect. His plan involves your dying and one day being raised to life again, being completely remade into a new version of you. However, God's idea of the perfect you may not be exactly the same as your idea of the perfect you.

My idea of the perfect me would involve having good tidy hair and a nice red convertible, preaching to packed halls, and being the ideal mother to a crowd of impeccably behaved and constantly happy children. But God is more interested in perfecting my inside than my outside. God has a plan to give me a nature like his own.

As Paul puts it, 'The fruit of the Spirit is love, joy, peace, patience, kindness, goodness, faithfulness, gentleness and self-control' (Galatians 5:22–23a). Being fruitful doesn't have to mean bearing children, making money or being popular. There are other types of fruit. The point of being fruitful is to grow and produce something. Instead of worrying about the fruit that you have not borne, you could try to spend a bit of time thinking about the fruit that you do bear. Which of the characteristics of the fruit of the Spirit can you identify in your own life? You could try keeping a 'Fruit Diary' for a week, noting at the end of each day any examples you can recall of the Spirit working in you to produce fruit. At the end of the week, you may find that you have a lot to thank God for, as well as some requests to make.

Although God works in us through the Holy Spirit to produce fruit, we ourselves can help or hinder this work. We can make an effort to try to practise more patience, kindness, gentleness and self-control. We can concentrate our own minds on love, joy, peace, goodness and faithfulness. There are many aspects of life that are out of our control, but we can work on ourselves.

One of the things that can make infertility hard to handle is the sense of a lack of control. It is possible that working on our self-control can help us to feel as though we are back in the driving-seat of our own lives. We can control our tempers, our speech and our actions.

If I look back over the past years, it can be tempting to think of all those months of 'trying to conceive' as wasted months, but, if I take time to examine the months properly, I usually find that they were not wasted at all. There are always things that I have achieved in that time. There are skills that I have learned or improved. I have taken up new tasks or kept on doing old ones. I don't spend all of my time trying to conceive. When I remember all that I have been doing, it helps me to forget about the one big thing that I haven't managed yet.

Now look back at your own nature and see if you can

recognise the fruit of the Spirit growing in your life. Has all the waiting helped you develop patience or faithfulness? Has responding to those who ask, 'Do you have any children?' helped you develop self-control? Has supporting your partner through this difficult time helped you develop love?

Part of being a Christian means growing in faith and getting closer to the nature of Christ himself. As time passes, as we pray, read the Bible and worship God, we will become more and more Christ-like. Now might be a good time to take stock of the changes that Christ has made in your life. Look back as far as you can remember and see how you have grown; see the fruit that you have borne.

Infertile and unsaved

And Adam was not the one deceived; it was the woman who was deceived and became a sinner. But women will be saved through childbearing—if they continue in faith, love and holiness with propriety. (1 TIMOTHY 2:14–15)

Communist Russia used to award a 'Mother Heroine' medal to women who had raised ten or more children. This sort of award makes it clear how high a value that society placed on reproduction. The verse from 1 Timothy above seems to be the Bible's version of this medal. It glorifies childbearing, appearing to claim that a woman's very salvation is linked to her ability to have a child.

Modern scholars, however, do not endorse this interpretation. In the *Expositor's Bible Commentary*, it is suggested that this verse may refer to Jesus, who was born to Mary and brought salvation into the world. We know from elsewhere in the Bible that we are saved through faith in Christ, not through any works of our own (see Ephesians 2:8–9). We also know that God has sympathy for infertile women and not condemnation (see Psalm 113).

Nonetheless, the importance of reproduction to society and to our own families cannot be ignored. The echoes of this thinking can linger, and you might feel as though you are not doing your duty by your family, your country or your faith because of your infertility. I do not think that the ideal of the fertile woman has vanished with the new way that society views women. Although women are now accepted in the workplace and are valued for other attributes, infertility is still considered a kind of failure. Personally, I found it particularly hard to be unable to present my parents in-law with a grandchild. Having married their son, I felt an old-fashioned call of duty to produce a grandchild. My continual failure to do so seemed to devalue me as a wife and as a daughter-in-law.

Infertility is not a modern problem; there have always been infertile couples. It was the fact of infertility that led to the idolatrous worship of mother goddess figures, such as Gaia and Isis. Despite our medical advances, fertility—or lack of it—can still be a mystery.

In fact, women who are not pregnant are the norm. Of course, a lot of women will conceive one day, but no woman is constantly pregnant. Even if you had no problem with infertility, you would still spend a very small fraction of your life actually being pregnant and giving birth. The image of the 'mother figure' is only an image, rather than a real woman whom you can imitate.

Mary, the mother of Christ, is traditionally held up as the ideal mother figure, as if she was constantly experiencing the same pregnancy over and over again—but we know that is not what happened. Her pregnancy is only a small part of her story, and it was her faith that was constant, not her pregnancy. When the angel greeted Mary for the first time, he said, 'Greetings, you who are highly favoured! The Lord is with you' (Luke 1:28). Mary's greatest blessing was not fertility; it was the presence of the Lord in her life. The angel characterises Mary as a woman blessed by God because of his presence with her, not because of her pregnancy.

Pregnancy lasts about nine months, which is a small proportion of anyone's life. Pregnancy and childbirth cannot be the main part or sole purpose of anyone's life. In being unable to bear children, we are not missing an entire life but only a small fraction of the many experiences that life has to offer. Even bringing up a child is not the only thing that anyone does. Most people don't even think about having children until their late teens or early 20s at the very earliest, but their lives are not empty and pointless before they have their children. Most people's children leave home around 20 years after they are born, but those parents do not then become useless and unfulfilled.

You already know this. Think about the people whom you like and admire. What do you like them for? What is it that you admire most about them? I would hazard a guess that you don't admire other people for their fertility. That would be absurd. You admire people for the way they live their lives and for what they have achieved. You may admire someone's parenting style but you would probably not admire someone who had nothing in their life apart from the ability to bear children. Indeed, you might pity such a person, because they would not be living a full life.

So, stop trying to become a fertility goddess and think of yourself as a fully rounded person! Think about the other aims in your life: perhaps you could take another step towards fulfilling them. You are more than just your infertility; therefore, remember and celebrate all the other things that make up your life.

Letting go of the perfect marriage

The gift of marriage brings husband and wife together
in the delight and tenderness of sexual union
and joyful commitment to the end of their lives.
It is given as the foundation of family life
in which children are born and nurtured
and in which each member of the family,
in good times and in bad,
may find strength, companionship and comfort,
and grow to maturity in love.[5]

There is more to marriage than the bearing of children. Infertile marriages are no less beautiful, no less important, no less life-giving and no less a picture of Christ and the Church than are fertile marriages.

Unless you are a very unusual person, you did not choose your husband or wife because you thought they would be particularly fertile. You chose to marry that particular person because they made you laugh, because they knew how to comfort you when you were sad, because you made a good team, because you understood each other. There were many reasons for you to marry the person that you married, and fertility was probably not even one of them.

Infertility doesn't change who you are fundamentally. All of the qualities that first drew you to one another are still there. They still draw you together. Your marriage can be just as wonderful as you hoped it would be, whether you have children or not. Your marriage can also be just as integral to the community, whether you have children or not. You can still be a stable unit; you can still be a team. You can still offer hospitality and set an example to all who meet you of what love looks like. Your marriage can still have purpose. It can still bear fruit.

It may be helpful to remember that there aren't any perfect marriages. All marriages have their faults, because marriages are made of people and all people have their faults. Also, all marriages will go through difficult times, because no relationship is a sequence of endless joys and pleasures. Into every marriage a little rain must fall.

In our marriage vows, we promise:

> ... *to have and to hold*
> *from this day forward;*
> *for better, for worse,*
> *for richer, for poorer,*
> *in sickness and in health,*
> *to love and to cherish,*
> *till death us do part.*[6]

When you got married, you promised to stay together, whatever the future held. Even on that happy day, the joyous beginning of your marriage, you were thinking about the possible trials that life had in store for you. When you stood there all dressed up, surrounded by family and friends, radiant with pleasure, you shared vows that talked about all the things that might go wrong. You did it because you knew that that was what marriage was about. The whole point of marriage is to be together through the tough times.

Any relationship can make it through the easy times. Any couple can be happy together when everything is going right: you don't need commitment to endure the good moments. You need commitment when the future looks bleak. You need commitment to hold you together when you can't agree, when suffering threatens to set you apart.

This moment, when you are having a difficult time, is what your marriage was made for. This is when your marriage demonstrates the point and purpose of the relationship. It is now that your marriage shows to the world, and to you, what love looks like. If you can hold on to each other now, if you continue to love and cherish each other, then you have the perfect marriage. Supporting each other if you can, huddling together to shelter from the storm of life at its worst—this is what 'fruitful marriage' means.

Letting go of the perfect future

I had names picked out for my future children. At the moment they were born, my husband was going to whisper in their ear, 'The Lord bless you and keep you; the Lord make his face shine upon you and be gracious to you; the Lord turn his face toward you and give you peace' (the blessing from Numbers 6:24–26), so that it would be the first thing they heard on entering the world. We had even considered the party that would follow their dedication service. We had talked about bedtimes and pocket money, schools and universities, how we wanted to bring them up and what we hoped their futures would hold.

There was a clear picture in my mind of the future I wanted. I read books about pregnancy and books about bringing up children. When I saw other people with their children, I would sometimes think, 'I'm so looking forward to doing that with my children', and sometimes, 'I would never do that with my child.' I thought I knew the kind of parent that I would be.

The apostle James wrote:

> Now listen, you who say, 'Today or tomorrow we will go to this or that city, spend a year there, carry on business and make money.' Why, you do not even know what will happen tomorrow. What is your life? You are a mist that appears for a little while and then vanishes. Instead, you ought to say, 'If it is the Lord's will, we will live and do this or that.' (JAMES 4:13–15)

Nobody knows what will happen in the future. Infertility is not the only way in which our plans for ourselves can be suddenly wiped out. There are many unforeseen circumstances, some good and some bad, which can completely change our plans.

Note that James doesn't say we shouldn't make plans. He simply says we should accept that our plans may be changed for us. We can only make plans based on the information that we have available. We do not know enough about the future to be sure of what will happen, so we make the best plans that we can, prayerfully and in line with what we learn about God's will from scripture.

I once heard a minister say that it is easier to steer a ship when it is moving than when it is still, so we should go ahead and try to do things, trusting that God will steer us in the right direction. I don't know much about steering ships, but I do know that it is bad for the car tyres if I try to steer when the car isn't moving, so I think I know what the minister meant. It is very hard to work out what God wants us to do, so often the best thing is to start going somewhere and trust that God will let us know if we are moving in the wrong direction.

Perhaps I am not meant to have children, and perhaps it is the strength of my desire that keeps me from hearing God's word on the matter. Perhaps, if I wanted children less, I would be more readily able to hear God's voice telling me that I am not meant to have them. I don't know. But I will keep doing what I am doing and I will pray that God makes his will clear to me in his own good time. We can be sure that if God is determined to say something to us, he will be able to make his voice heard.

It is not easy to accept that your perfect future is not to be. Those children whom I planned for and whose names I had selected are almost like real children to me. In failing to acquire those children, I have lost something that I thought I had. People who have children with unexpected disabilities sometimes find that they have to mourn for the children they might have had before they can easily rejoice in the children they have now. There is a loss for them to mourn as well as a gain for them to celebrate. I have had to mourn for my lost children—those imagined children that I thought I was going to have. It is not a physical loss because I never actually held them; they never were real. But it is a loss none the less.

Father God, I am grieving;
I feel as though I have lost a possible future.
Please help me to let go of my plans.
I know that it is your place to make big plans and not mine.
Please help me to remember
that you are the creator and sustainer of all.

It is only by your will that I get up in the morning,
It is only by your will that the earth keeps turning.
Please help me to trust in you. Amen

✳ CHAPTER 7 ✳

Loving and being loved

'It drives my husband crazy. He can't understand why I'm so miserable all the time. He just wants me to get over it.'

'Sex isn't the same any more It's just something we do on schedule. When it's over, I feel relieved that I can tick it off my to-do list.'

'What if he leaves me for someone who can have children?'

'At a family gathering, my husband was playing with some little children and one of his aunts asked me, "Why don't you give him a son of his own?" I feel like I'm letting everyone down and failing to be a proper wife.'

'He used to call me "baby" as a pet name, but I can't stand to hear it any more.'

'Every time we try to have a conversation, we end up talking about the baby thing.'

Elkanah her husband would say to her, 'Hannah, why are you weeping? Why don't you eat? Why are you down-hearted? Don't I mean more to you than ten sons?'

(1 Samuel 1:8).

When I read this passage, my heart goes out to Elkanah. It is terrible to see your spouse grieving over something that you cannot help. For many of us, one of the hardest aspects of infertility will be watching our spouse suffer infertility. It is one thing to have our own sorrow; it is quite another to watch our partner grieve.

It can make us feel insecure and insufficient because we probably don't like to think that we ourselves are not enough to bring a smile to our partner's face. Even if we do want to share children with our partner, few of us would like to think that we were less important to them than a child who doesn't exist yet. Shouldn't we mean more to them than ten imaginary sons? Are you married to a Hannah? Do you find yourself longing to hear them say, 'Yes, you are enough! I don't mind that there's no baby. I have you and that is enough.'

Maybe it's the other way around. Maybe you are the one who cannot stop grieving and it is your partner who feels inadequate. Are you married to an Elkanah? What do you say when they ask, 'Aren't I enough for you?' There may well be a part of you that would like to say, 'Of course you are enough for me: you're my life-partner, my soulmate; you're enough!'

It wasn't what you expected, however. You expected that your love for one another would result in a baby. 'When a mummy and daddy love each other very, very much, they have a special hug and that's where babies come from.' We have probably all heard that simple explanation. It may even resemble the way that your parents explained sex to you when you were a child. The words can hover for ever in our minds: 'When a mummy and daddy love each other very, very much…'

First comes love,
Then comes marriage,
Then along comes the baby carriage.
A PLAYGROUND RHYME

We are led to expect that love will lead to a baby. Our love for one another is supposed to result in a new life, so wanting a baby is not a rejection of your partner. If your partner wants a baby, they are not rejecting you. Rather, they want your shared love to blossom and to bear the fruit of a new life.

We need to be aware of the effect that infertility can have on a marriage. Infertility forces us to watch our partner grieve and it can easily lead us to Elkanah's state of mind. We can find ourselves distressed by our partner's sorrow and asking, 'Aren't I enough?' If our marriage is going to survive the storm of infertility, we have to protect it and put some effort into building it up.

In the following pages, you may want to skip to the sections that particularly interest you, or you may wish to read every one. Marriage is a complicated organism in which everything is connected to everything else, so there is some overlap between different sections. I have divided them up more for ease of reading than because I think marriage can be divided into five neat and discrete sections.

Keeping your sex life going

The wife's body does not belong to her alone but also to her husband. In the same way, the husband's body does not belong to him alone but also to his wife. Do not deprive each other except by mutual consent and for a time, so that you may devote yourselves to prayer. Then come together again so that Satan will not tempt you because of your lack of self-control. (1 CORINTHIANS 7:4–5)

Your sex life is an important aspect of your marriage. In *Let's Make Love*, Jack Dominion writes:

> In marriage, the couple has their own domestic church and at the centre of this church is the enactment of sexual intercourse. Sexual intercourse as a divine liturgy gives the couple the means to experience and create love.[7]

It's not called 'making love' for nothing.

The procreation of children isn't the sole purpose of sex. Sex is also given to us as a way of binding husband and wife together, helping them to build a strong marriage. It should be one aspect of the joy and pleasure that your marriage brings you. It should also be a consolation in difficult times, yet my husband and I found that, at various stages during our journey of infertility, our sex life became miserable and joyless.

The first problem is that sex can be a reminder of failure. Sometimes it is hard to put conception out of your mind while you are having sex with your partner. My husband couldn't stand it if I made any reference to conceiving while we were making love. He said (quite understandably) that it ruined the mood for him.

The second problem is that some fertility treatments may involve changing aspects of your sex life. You may, for example, be required to make love at certain times and abstain at others. Making love to a schedule can make it very hard to enjoy your sex life.

Here are the ways in which we restored the joy and pleasure to our sex life.

- Allow yourselves plenty of time for sex. This is especially important if you *have* to have sex on a certain day. Don't try to fit it into a ten-minute window before you fall asleep. Maybe, some months, you could book a day off work so that you can enjoy some quality time together. Go to bed an hour (or several hours) early and spend some time working up to the main event. Alternatively, you could try waking up early so that you can take your time making love early in the morning.
- Try something a bit different—a different room or a new position. You could go shopping in an adult store (online if you're shy) and buy something you've never used before. You could tell each other your fantasies and try acting them out. Buy new underwear; have a bath or a shower together; give each other a massage. Sex is supposed to be a pleasure, not a chore, so see if you can find a new aspect that you both enjoy.
- Talk to each other. Remember that your bodies belong to one another, so what happens with your body is your partner's business (and vice versa). Tell each other what feels good and what doesn't. Work out what helps your partner get in the mood for sex: talking, going to watch a film, having a bath, laughing together, waiting the whole day for the pleasure of holding each other. If you're going to be close, you need to communicate.
- If things are really bad, ask for help. Your GP or fertility consultant will have dealt with this before. You are not the first couple to experience a dip in your sex life, to find the

stress of infertility affecting your sexual relationship. This is an important aspect of your marriage, too important to be ignored.

Having said all that, it doesn't help to worry too much about your sex life, either. Very few couples find that sex remains as exciting as it was on their honeymoon throughout the whole of their marriage. The good news is that, for most married couples, there are fantastic peaks in which the sex is great. The bad news is that most married couples also experience troughs in which the sex is less frequent or less satisfying.

Whatever you do to help keep your sex life going, try to do it together. Paul wrote that you shouldn't deprive one another except by mutual agreement (1 Corinthians 7:5), but it is also true that you shouldn't drastically increase the tempo except by mutual agreement. Only a very limited amount of surprise is a good thing in the bedroom. Your partner is unlikely to thank you for turning your bedroom into an 18+ movie without warning them.

The Bible contains quite a lot of advice on making love. The basic points are: get to know your partner, value their pleasure, know your body, and take your time. It is fashionable to consider Song of Songs to be about the divine love that God has for us, but it also contains a lot of very down-to-earth advice about how to have a satisfying sex life.

The lover and the beloved spend long passages describing their own and one another's bodies—with creativity and imagination, with great appreciation, but also with detail. They have clearly taken time to get to know one another's bodies, as well as their own. This is key to a good sex life.

How beautiful you are, my darling!
Oh, how beautiful!
Your eyes behind your veil are doves.
Your hair is like a flock of goats
descending from Mount Gilead.
Your teeth are like a flock of sheep just shorn,
coming up from the washing.
Each has its twin;
not one of them is alone.
Your lips are like a scarlet ribbon;
your mouth is lovely.
Your temples behind your veil
are like the halves of a pomegranate.
Your neck is like the tower of David,
built with elegance;
on it hang a thousand shields,
all of them shields of warriors.
Your two breasts are like two fawns,
like twin fawns of a gazelle
that browse among the lilies.   (SONG OF SONGS 4:1–5)

This is an interesting description. It is obviously meant to be admiring, although it is hard to imagine anyone, these days, being flattered by having their teeth compared to sheep. But perhaps the sweet nothings between lovers shouldn't make sense to anyone outside the relationship. My favourite part of my body happens to be my collar bones and my husband frequently comments on how prominent my clavicles are, but this is not something that I would expect everyone to take as a compliment. The ability to compliment our lover is almost as much about knowing their personality as it is about knowing their body.

I notice that the lover starts with the eyes, takes in the rest of the face, then moves down the neck to the breasts. That is not an instruction manual for every sexual encounter but it does illustrate the importance of focusing on 'public' parts of the body as well as 'private' parts. Don't make the mistake of thinking that knowing your partner's body is all about staring at their bottom, any more than it's all about staring into their eyes. As someone's sexual partner, you are the only one who sees every little bit of them. Appreciate the gift they have given you in allowing you, and you only, to take possession of their body. Take your time and enjoy building a sense of ownership of your partner's body.

The old marriage vows contain the promise, 'With my body, I thee worship.' This isn't intended to sound idolatrous; it is used in the sense of 'giving honour'. It is something that we should still try to do when we are intimate with one another (even when we're not in the act of sex itself). If we use our body to honour our partner's body—taking our time, giving pleasure to different parts—then we will be on our way to pleasurable sex for both parties. If our partner's body is also our body, then we should value their arousal as much as we value our own. Great sex can come from focusing on your partner's needs and trying to meet them.

I slept but my heart was awake.
Listen! My lover is knocking:
'Open to me, my sister, my darling,
my dove, my flawless one.
My head is drenched with dew,
my hair with the dampness of the night.'
I have taken off my robe—
must I put it on again?

I have washed my feet—
must I soil them again?
My lover thrust his hand through the latch-opening;
my heart began to pound for him.
I arose to open for my lover,
and my hands dripped with myrrh,
my fingers with flowing myrrh,
on the handles of the lock.   (Song of Songs 5:2–5)

I love this scene. It illustrates perfectly the teamwork required to make sex successful and pleasurable for both partners. Despite not really being in the mood, the beloved gets up and responds to her lover's advances. The meeting of their hands—his hand reaching in, her hand opening—is a perfect picture of a couple responding to each other, moving together, bringing their bodies together to create mutual pleasure.

Continuing to have fun together

Infertility can consume a great deal of your thought-life. You may find that it intrudes on all sorts of moments when you would rather not be thinking about it. For example, my husband and I used to enjoy visiting aquariums. He grew up by the sea, so he could recognise all sorts of British fish, and I was slowly learning to recognise some of them. When I was going through a low patch and feeling particularly sensitive about my infertility, however, I found that visiting aquariums was much less pleasant. Seeing other couples enjoying a day out with their children reminded me of what I was missing. Every time I saw someone cradling a baby or pushing a pram, I experienced a painful jolt as I remembered that I couldn't have children. Sometimes it makes sense to think ahead and try to protect yourself from seeing too many happy families. We found that staying away from large visitor attractions during school holidays and not attending the cinema until late in the evening were good ways to avoid seeing children when we were feeling fragile.

Fertility treatments may also take up a large proportion of your time. If you are seeing a doctor or a consultant, you may have to take time off work for these appointments, leaving you with less free time to enjoy together as a couple. If you are also trying holistic therapy or attending an infertility support group, you can easily find your time being eaten up by infertility-related activities.

It is important to remember the bigger picture. When you decided to start trying for a baby, you didn't decide to exchange your marriage for a child. If the child is taking a long time in coming, that's all the more reason to ensure that you keep your marriage together.

Make space in your mind for thoughts other than infertility. I started reading romance novels, which gave my mind a different focus and had the added benefit of reminding me how lucky I am to have found the man with whom I want to spend the rest of my life. If your mind keeps returning to infertility, you may need to find a distraction. The world is full of exciting things to do and new things to learn. Try to stop yourself from focusing on and limiting your experiences to just one small aspect.

Make space in your life for activities that are nothing to do with having a baby. Go to the theatre or the cinema, or go out for dinner. Nicky and Sila Lee, in *The Marriage Book*, recommend that all married couples have a 'date night' once a week, when you book an evening to spend together doing something that you will enjoy, taking it in turns to plan what to do. One week, you might take a walk around your local area on a Wednesday night. Another week, your partner might bring you breakfast in bed on a Saturday morning. I don't think that the 'date night' has to resemble the dates you used to go on before you were married (although, one week, that might be a nice change). The idea is to make time to do special things together and create happy memories. When you look back at this period of your marriage in five or ten years' time, you will want to have happy memories to relive rather than remembering nothing but trying to conceive.

To keep the fun alive in your marriage, you may need to try these four prongs of attack. Think of your sorrow as an enemy that you can and will defeat together. Attack it on several fronts at once and you will see your marriage triumph.

First, allow yourselves plenty of time together. When you were first getting to know one another, you probably met up whenever you could, you talked on the phone, and you emailed and exchanged letters. You knew then that it took time to get to know someone new. When you first got married, you probably continued to spend lots of time together. You made an effort to hurry home after work so that you could eat together; you put aside time to work on the house together and to determine the fair shares of housework. You knew then that it would take time to learn how to live comfortably together. Now, you are not the same people as when you first married, so allow yourselves time to get to know one another again. You need to adjust to the fact of infertility in your lives, just as you needed to adjust to the change of marriage, so allow yourselves time to work out how you are going to tackle this new complication.

Second, try something a bit different. A new project like tidying up the garden or redecorating the bedroom will give you something to focus on as a team and will allow you (eventually) a great sense of achievement. How about taking an evening class together at your local college? Your church may run Bible study groups that you could start attending together. You could try reading poetry to one another or spending weekends painting side-by-side. If you try something that you haven't done before, you may discover a new hobby or skill as well as rediscovering the pleasure of one another's company.

Third, talk to each other. In the early days, I am sure, talking made up a huge part of your relationship. When we have been in a relationship for a long time, however, we can find ourselves making less of an effort. It can sometimes feel as though you already know each other so well that there's nothing left to say—but there is always something to say. Talk about the details of your day. Discuss the dreams that you had as children. Rank all the music you like or all the films you've ever seen. Nobody knows anyone completely, so make it your aim to find out some new things about your partner and to tell them some things that they don't yet know about you. When you've done all that, reminisce together. One of the joys of a long marriage is that you have so many shared memories. Start with the day you met and see if you can remember what first attracted you to each other. Tell each other about the highlights of your marriage so far. As you remember all the great times that you have had, you will be thankful once again for your wonderful marriage.

Fourth, again, if things are really bad, ask for help. Some problems in marriages cannot be fixed by taking a walk together and making an effort to have lunch together once a week. If your marriage is struggling, you don't need to struggle on alone. Nicky and Sila Lee have written *The*

Marriage Course as well as *The Marriage Book*: a church near you may run a course that you could join. The Relate organisation offers counselling to couples who are having trouble in their marriage: contact details are at the back of this book. Your church minister or pastoral team should be able to help you find the right support for your marriage. Remember that during your marriage service (if it took place in a church), the congregation will have promised to help and support your marriage in the years to come. Even if your wedding wasn't a church wedding, all those who attended were there to express their support for your relationship. If your marriage needs support, now is the time to take them up on that offer.

Supporting and being supported

The whole point of your marriage is that you are a source of support to one another. You are to work as a team, helping each other to achieve your God-given goals. If you do manage to have a baby, you will need to support each other as parents, so it's a good idea to start practising now.

Before I was married, I read *The Five Love Languages* by Gary Chapman. Chapman has a theory that there are five different ways of communicating love. If your partner doesn't speak the same 'love language' as you, they may not feel the love that you are trying to show them. We can all fall into the trap of assuming that our partner knows how we feel. It can be helpful to stop and check that your partner is receiving the message of love from you. You might want to think about the different ways in which you express love for your partner and the different ways in which your partner expresses love for you.

Just as you need to support your partner, so your partner needs to support you. There are two sides to every marriage and both sides need to be working. When you try to support your partner, you may notice that they can make it easier or harder for you, depending on how they respond to your overtures of support and love. If they put up a wall around themselves and refuse to discuss their feelings with you, it can be hard to support them; but if your partner thanks you for a special effort that you have made, it can be easier to find the energy to go on making that special effort. You can help or hinder your partner in exactly the same way. You can put up walls that make it hard for your partner's love to get through to you. Conversely, you can give them a sense of success that will spur them on to continue supporting you.

Walls that hinder support include lack of communication, lack of enthusiasm and lack of empathy.

We have already touched on the issue of communication but it is important enough to be repeated: if you don't talk to your partner, that makes it hard for them to say anything nice to you. If you don't tell them about your feelings, that makes it hard for them to consider your feelings. If you don't give any feedback on their attempts to express love for you, they may think that you don't notice or don't care what they are doing.

Lack of enthusiasm can also be a wall that stops your partner's love and support from reaching you. Imagine that your partner has gone to a great deal of trouble to arrange a surprise birthday party for you, secretly contacting your friends and inviting them all to your house. You get home from an errand to find 50 of your closest family and friends leaping out and shouting, 'Surprise!' Now imagine that your response was not gratitude, but anger that the food wasn't exactly as you would have planned it and the decorations not quite to your taste. How would your partner feel? Would they ever throw you a surprise party again?

Of course, you and I are nice, reasonable people who appreciate it when our partners do nice things for us, but all of us can be guilty of receiving our partner's love with something less than enthusiasm at times. We have all shrugged off a hug when we didn't feel like it or given a poorly chosen present a cool reception. If we respond with lacklustre enthusiasm to our partner's expressions of love and support, however, they may feel it as a rebuff and be less inclined to show love and support in future.

The final type of wall is the one put up by a lack of empathy. It is easy to rebuff our partner's signs of love if we don't recognise those signs. If we don't understand what they are trying to do, we will find it very hard to appreciate the love that they are trying to express.

This doesn't mean that we are expected to read our partner's mind. My parents have an uncanny ability to do this when playing cards, and it makes it very hard to play bridge against them. But in everyday life, most people cannot guess what their partner is thinking for much of the time. The Bible describes a married couple as sharing their bodies, not their minds. This means that we should make an effort to try to understand where our partner is coming from. The longer we are married, the easier it will be to understand the background to their actions and decisions, because, as our marriage goes on, more and more of our past will be a past that we share with our partner. However, if we don't understand what is going on in their head, we should still ask them, however long we have known them.

Ultimately we all know a lot about whatever is important

to us. If you value your partner, you will find them interesting and you will learn a lot about them without really noticing that you're doing it. I have a friend who knows the entire score of *Les Misérables*. He never sat down and deliberately learned it all, but he enjoys listening to it. So he listened to it a lot, he went to see the show several times and, without deliberately intending to do so, he learned the entire thing. You can learn about your partner in just the same way.

All of this will help us to recognise when our partner is demonstrating their love for us. When we recognise that they are trying to show us love, we will probably find that we feel loved and supported.

Of course, there are other walls that can be put up to prevent love reaching us. You may have designed some special customised ones of your own. Sadly, the walls that we put up to stop ourselves getting hurt are the same walls that stop us feeling loved. It can be hard work to pull them down, especially for those of us who have suffered a lot of hurt in the past.

Finally, when we have worked on clearing the way for our partner's love to reach us, we will be able to encourage them to keep on loving us. Most people like to be thanked when they have made a special effort. Your partner will probably appreciate it if you thank them for some of the expressions of love that they make towards you.

Being supported is something that takes practice, just as being supportive does.

At our wedding, my husband and I had this reading from Ecclesiastes 4:9–12:

Two are better than one,
because they have a good return for their work:

if one falls down,
his friend can help him up.
But pity the man who falls
and has no one to help him up!
Also, if two lie down together, they will keep warm.
But how can one keep warm alone?
Though one may be overpowered,
two can defend themselves.
A cord of three strands is not quickly broken.

In marriage, the two of you can offer one another a great deal of support, love and comfort. Ultimately, though, if your marriage is to be strong and lasting, you will need a third strand to hold the two of you together and to offer the support that you cannot give one another. The third strand is God, who lives in you and in your partner and works between you, keeping you loving and supporting and drawing you ever closer together and to him.

God's love

Dear friends, let us love one another, for love comes from God. Everyone who loves has been born of God and knows God. Whoever does not love does not know God, because God is love. This is how God showed his love among us: he sent his one and only Son into the world that we might live through him. This is love: not that we loved God, but that he loved us and sent his Son as an atoning sacrifice for our sins. Dear friends, since God so loved us, we also ought to love one another. No one has ever seen God; but if we love one another, God lives in us and his love is made complete in us.   (1 JOHN 4:7–12)

God is the only source of love; all the love that we have to give to him, or to other people, comes from God. It was God who made the first move, creating us to love him, then sending his own Son to die so that we could be reconciled to him. Even when we are feeling empty and unable to love anyone, God sends us his love. We do not need to make the first move with God. We do not need to travel far down the road towards him before we will find him (just like the father of the prodigal son) running to meet us with open arms.

Infertility and disappointment may make us feel empty, but God fills us with his love. He chooses to live inside us so that we need not be empty. We can be filled with God's love.

We cannot destroy love either, because God is love. We will not run out of love for our partner or our family or our church or our friends. God has an inexhaustible supply of love; it is his very being. So it is that when we love others, God makes our love complete. He ensures that none of our love is wasted.

God loves us, so we receive love. Then we can love others, so transferring the love on to someone else. We cannot be the beginning of the energy chain of love; it always starts with God, but we can move love about and transfer it into others or back to God. It is only God, however, in whom love is made complete; and when we love God, all of the love that we have for him is received by him, because God is inside us. He knows what we are thinking and feeling before we are aware of it ourselves.

That's why we need God's help to have a good and fulfilling marriage. All that extra love has to come from somewhere, and God will supply us with all the love that we need to support our partner.

At the opening of this chapter, we saw Hannah weeping

and her husband Elkanah unable to soothe her. That is not where the Bible leaves her, however. Hannah takes her sorrow to God and prays: 'In bitterness of soul Hannah wept much and prayed to the Lord' (1 Samuel 1:10). Hannah pours out her bitterness, her sorrow and her disappointment, alone before God. Then she goes home.

The next day, she is back with her family. They worship God together, and then Hannah and Elkanah are reunited as husband and wife and make love together: 'Then she went her way and ate something, and her face was no longer downcast. Early the next morning they arose and worshipped before the Lord and then went back to their home at Ramah. Elkanah lay with Hannah his wife' (vv. 18–19).

Spending time alone with God, sharing her heart with him, gives Hannah strength to return to her husband and love him once more. She returns from her time of private prayer refreshed and no longer downcast. Time alone with God can lift our spirits and restore our souls. The love that God has for us shields us from the pains and sorrows of life and makes them easier to bear.

Spending time together, worshipping God, unites Elkanah and Hannah and sends them off full of love to share with one another. When we remember together God's love, we are better able to love each other. Like Hannah, we too can take our burdens to God when our sorrow is getting in the way of our relationships with others. We too can stand with our partners and worship God together when we need help to love one another. Spending time with God, whether alone or with our partner, helps us to love our partner and to feel their love for us. That is what John meant when he wrote, 'Everyone who loves has been born of God and knows God.'

Father God, I am in love.
Thank you for giving me a partner to share my life with.
Sometimes it's hard work sharing love with someone.
Please help me learn how to love and how to be loved.
I know that all love comes from you
and it is only through you that we can love one another.
Please help me to let your love flow through me to my partner.
Amen

CHAPTER 8

Obsession

'I can't think about anything else.'

'It distracts me all the time.'

'I can't bear to make any plans for the future, just in case a baby comes along.'

Very few of us live in the present. We can spend a lot of our time thinking about the past, looking back in pleasure or anger at what we have done and what others have done. We can also spend a lot of time thinking about the future, looking forward to what might be and making plans of what we would like to see happen. We tend to spend very little time thinking about the present, where we are now and what we are currently doing.

Do not worry about tomorrow

When trying for a baby, we are bound to devote a lot of thought to our possible futures. Maybe you think about whether you might have a boy or a girl; maybe you make plans for leaving work or starting to work part-time. Almost certainly, you will find yourself thinking. 'Will it work this month? Will I have a baby before Christmas? Will this be the last summer holiday we have together, just the two of us?' These thoughts are natural but they are not helpful.

Christmas, birthdays and even the passing of the seasons can become no more than reminders of how long your suffering is lasting. In this way, annual celebrations can become a source of pain rather than a source of pleasure.

If your attempts to conceive a child have gone on for some time, the passing of time will probably have become very painful to you. Every month that passes is another failure; every Christmas is another Christmas without a child of your own; every birthday marks another year of childlessness. So you may easily find yourself thinking, 'This will be the last month of failure. This will be the last lonely Christmas. This will be the last childless birthday.' You may often find yourself looking forward to an event that seems a long way off—six months from now, one year from now, two years from now—and promising yourself that you will be a parent by then. There is no good in doing this and it may well cause you a great deal more pain.

Try not to look too far ahead. Try not to promise yourself that you will have a baby by such-and-such a date. You cannot keep such a promise, and we should never make promises that we cannot keep, especially not to ourselves. If you do manage to get pregnant, none of these deadlines will matter any more. If you don't, the deadlines will cause you to feel worse because they will be a sign of your continued failure to conceive.

This doesn't mean that you can't make any future plans. You must continue to live your life and you must book next year's holiday, decide whether you want to move house, or save up to buy a new car. You must make plans for your future, but you cannot plan for when you will have a family. Don't set yourself deadlines for things that you cannot achieve.

Ecclesiastes 3:11a says, 'He has made everything beautiful

in its time.' When you type a password into your computer, the password will usually be case-sensitive, which means that some of the letters are supposed to be UPPER CASE and others are supposed to be lower case. You may be typing in all the same letters, but, unless you put them in the correct case, the computer will not recognise your password. God's plan for the universe and his plan for us are time-sensitive plans. There are some things that are very good at one time but not so good at another time. It may seem to us as though our having a baby ought to be a very good thing, but it might not be a very good thing at this time, from God's perspective.

It is important to remember that just because this moment of time is a childless moment, that does not mean it is an empty moment. There are other things going on at this moment that are good. There are other important tasks for you to be doing at this moment, besides bearing children. Even sorrow is beautiful in its time.

Each day has enough trouble of its own

One of the biggest problems with living in the future is the tendency to put off other activities and decisions. You might tell yourself that right now you will concentrate on getting pregnant and, later, when you have the baby, you will think about getting more involved in church activities. You might tell yourself that now, while you are struggling with infertility, your marriage is taking a bit of a beating, but once you're pregnant you'll be able to concentrate on being a good wife. You may think that now, while you are having such a difficult time, you can't be a supportive friend, but once you have your family sorted out, you will have lots of energy to devote to your friendships.

However, these thoughts are not about taking care of yourself; they are actually about putting off what you know you ought to be doing. This has been a big problem for me. I haven't always wanted to do things while I am still infertile. For example, I wanted to wait until I had a baby before I got on with training for the ministry. Then I read this passage:

> Do not withhold good from those who deserve it
> when it is in your power to act.
> Do not say to your neighbour,
> 'Come back later; I'll give it tomorrow'—
> when you now have it with you.　　　(PROVERBS 3:27–28)

This reminded me that if I can do something now, then now is the time to do it. So I spoke to my minister about training for the ministry and I began to preach. For the last few years, I have been a lay preacher. I have stopped waiting for my infertility to be over and begun to serve God in my current state. I am no longer putting off my vocation until tomorrow; I am choosing to pursue it today.

It may sound a little vain to apply this passage to my lay preaching: I am not quite certain that I would be withholding good if I failed to preach! But the point is this: if you can do something right now, then you should do it right now, not wait until some indefinite time in the future. Remember, again, that there is more than one way of bearing fruit. If you cannot have a baby, that is all the more reason to get on with serving God in other ways. It is not an excuse to do nothing.

In his Sermon on the Mount, Jesus taught:

'Therefore I tell you, do not worry about your life, what you will eat or drink; or about your body, what you will wear. Is not life more important than food, and the body more important than clothes? Look at the birds of the air; they do not sow or reap or store away in barns, and yet your heavenly Father feeds them. Are you not much more valuable than they? Who of you by worrying can add a single hour to his life?

'And why do you worry about clothes? See how the lilies of the field grow. They do not labour or spin. Yet I tell you that not even Solomon in all his splendour was dressed like one of these. If that is how God clothes the grass of the field, which is here today and tomorrow is thrown into the fire, will he not much more clothe you, O you of little faith? So do not worry, saying, "What shall we eat?" or "What shall we drink?" or "What shall we wear?" For the pagans run after all these things, and your heavenly Father knows that you need them. But seek first his kingdom and his righteousness, and all these things will be given to you as well. Therefore do not worry about tomorrow, for tomorrow will worry about itself. Each day has enough trouble of its own.'   (MATTHEW 6:25–34)

This passage can be applied to all of our worries, and it can very easily be applied to infertility. Here is my own paraphrase:

'Therefore I tell you, do not worry about your life, whether you will ever be a parent; or about your body, if there is anything that can help you get pregnant. Is not life more than just having a child, and the body more than just a

131

walking womb? Look at the birds of the air; they don't panic about whether their eggs will hatch, and yet your heavenly Father ensures that their species continues. Are you not much more valuable than they? Who of you by worrying can increase their fertility?

'And why do you worry about whether you will get pregnant this month? See how the lilies of the field grow. They do not buy ovulation testing kits. Yet the world has never run out of flowers. If that is how much attention God pays to plants, which don't even have feelings or faith, will he not much more care for you, O you of little faith? So do not worry, saying, "What shall happen to us?" or "Will I get pregnant?" or "When will I have a child?" For the pagans run after all these things, and your heavenly Father knows that you want them. But seek first his kingdom and his righteousness, and all these things will be given to you as well. Therefore do not worry about tomorrow, for tomorrow will worry about itself. Each day has enough trouble of its own.'

God knows all about your sorrow: there is absolutely no point in worrying. You can trust that God has got the situation well in hand. Do you really think that the God who created the whole world would forget about your fertility? He knows what he is doing and you can safely trust him. In the meantime, today you do not have a baby and today you are not pregnant. It is enough for you to get on with the work that you have to do today.

It is also enough for you to cope with the sorrow that you bear today, without borrowing sorrow from tomorrow as well. It is dangerous to wonder about how you will cope if you *never* get pregnant, or even to worry about what will happen if you don't get pregnant next year.

Remember that throughout their time in the desert, God gave the Israelites enough manna to last them for a day at a time (Exodus 16:4–35). When each next day came, he fed them again. So it is with us. We have enough strength each day to get through the day. Tomorrow we will find the strength to get through tomorrow. If, indeed, you never get pregnant, you will get through that as it comes. 'For ever' is just a very long series of tomorrows, each of which you will be able to handle one day at a time.

Father God, I find it hard to get the right perspective on life.
Please help me not to worry about tomorrow.
I know that I can trust you.
Please help me to see what's going on around me.
I want to see you working in my life.
Please open my eyes. Amen

Further resources

Gary Chapman, *The Five Love Languages* (Moody, 2010).

Marilyn Crawshaw and Rachel Balen, *Adopting after Infertility* (Jessica Kingsley, 2010).

Jack Dominion, *Let's Make Love* (DLT, 2001).

Jean Gibson, *Seasons of Womanhood: Stories of despair and hope* (Authentic Media, 2007).

Janet Jaffe, *Unsung Lullabies* (St Martin's Griffin, 2005).

Timothy Jones, *The Art of Prayer: Conversations with God* (SU, 2006).

Nicky and Sila Lee, *The Marriage Book* (Alpha International, 2009).

C.S. Lewis, *The Great Divorce* (HarperCollins, 2002).

C.S. Lewis, *The Problem of Pain* (HarperCollins, 2002).

Jennifer Lord, *Adopting a Child* (BAAF, 2008).

Ann Morris, *The Adoption Experience: Families who give children a second chance* (Jessica Kingsley, 1999).

Jeanne Safer, *Beyond Motherhood: Choosing a life without children* (Paramount, 1996).

Matthew Taylor and Laurie Taylor, *What Are Children For?* (Short Books, 2003).

Robert Winston, *A Child Against All Odds* (Bantam, 2006).

Philip Yancey, *What's so Amazing about Grace?* (Zondervan, 2002).

Useful organisations and websites

Adoption UK
www.adoptionuk.org

BAAF (the British Association of Adoption and Fostering)
www.baaf.org

BICA (the British Infertility Counselling Association)
www.bica.net

COTS (Childlessness Overcome Through Surrogacy)
www.surrogacy.org.uk

Fertility Friends
www.fertilityfriends.co.uk

Kidding Aside: The British Childfree Association
www.kiddingaside.net

Relate
www.relate.org.uk

Notes

1. Actually, that simple fact does put infertility into a better perspective. The biblical writers didn't think that Jesus' marital status or fertility was worthy of any mention at all. Nor does my infertility have to define me.

2. Edward Albee, *Who's Afraid of Virginia Woolf?* (1962)

3. C.S. Lewis, *The Great Divorce* (Signature Classics, HarperCollins, 2002), p. 116.

4. Richard Dawkins, *River out of Eden* (Basic Books, 1995), p. 3.

5. From the introduction to the Marriage Service, *Common Worship: Pastoral Services*, (CHP, 2000).

6. From the Marriage Service, *Common Worship: Pastoral Services*.

7. Jack Dominion, *Let's Make Love* (DLT, 2001), p. 80.

Growing a Caring Church

Practical guidelines for pastoral care

Wendy Billington

In every church, of every size, meeting people's pastoral needs is a core area of ministry. If leadership resources are already stretched, however, it can be all too easy to fall short, with potentially disastrous consequences. We may notice and feel compassion when we see somebody struggling in some way, but we also need to be properly equipped in order to offer the kind of wise and practical assistance that will start to guide them back towards wholeness of life.

Earthed in Jesus' command that as his disciples we are to love one another, this book shows how home groups can be places where people's pain and difficulties are noticed, and first steps taken to help. Wendy Billington offers valuable insights coupled with down-to-earth advice, drawing on her years of pastoral work in the community and in the local church, as well as on her personal experiences of loss and cancer.

ISBN 978 1 84101 799 0   £6.99
Available from your local Christian bookshop or, in case of difficulty, direct from BRF: please visit www.brfonline.org.uk.

Also from BRF

Shaping the Heart

Reflections on spiritual formation and fruitfulness

Pamela Evans

God created the human heart to be a worship-filled, holy place with himself in residence, a garden in which the fruit of the Spirit may grow. *Shaping the Heart* is a book for every Christian who wants their heart to become—through the healing and redemptive touch of heavenly grace and mercy—a place where God delights to dwell.

Shaping the Heart is designed for practical use, whether as individual reading for a retreat or quiet day or for shared study and discussion in a group setting. The book considers different aspects of our lives in the light of Christian teaching and looks at how God can touch and transform us through his Spirit, so that we become fruitful disciples. Chapters conclude with three Bible reflections as a springboard to further prayer and reflection.

ISBN 978 1 84101 726 6   £7.99
Available from your local Christian bookshop or direct from BRF: visit www.brfonline.org.uk

Writing the Icon
of the Heart

In silence beholding

Maggie Ross

In *Writing the Icon of the Heart*, we are invited to share the reflections of one who, over the years, has spent long hours in silence and prayer in one of the world's most wild and solitary landscapes, as well as the more urban context of Oxford. Casting new and often startling light on ancient texts and long-established spiritual practices, Maggie Ross shows how faith cannot be divorced from an outlook characterised by a rigorous questioning and testing of assumptions, and a passionate concern for the created world in which we are blessed to live.

ISBN 978 1 84101 878 2   £6.99

Available from your local Christian bookshop or, in case of difficulty, direct from BRF: please visit www.brfonline.org.uk.

'Maggie Ross invites us into real quiet, which is also real presence, presence to ourselves and to the threefold mystery that eludes our concepts and even our ordinary ideas of "experience". A really transformative book.' (Archbishop Rowan Williams)

Walking with Gospel Women

Interactive Bible meditations

Fiona Stratta

Imaginative meditation can be a powerful way of attuning ourselves to God's presence, involving the emotions as well as the mind. This book offers a refreshing and inspiring way into Bible study, using meditative monologues based around many of the women of the Gospels. Through a time of guided reflection, we identify with the woman concerned and see what lessons emerge for today as we ponder her story.

Each chapter consists of a monologue, linked Bible passage and discussion material designed to draw out deep communication and group fellowship, as well as transformational learning. While designed primarily for small groups, the monologues can also be used as a way into silent reflection either for individuals or with larger groups.

ISBN 978 0 85746 010 3   £7.99
Available from your local Christian bookshop or, in case of difficulty, direct from BRF: please visit www.brfonline.org.uk.

Also available for Kindle

Dreaming of Home

Homecoming as a model for renewal and mission

Michael Mitton

Finding a sense of 'home', a special place of acceptance and belonging, is a fundamental human longing. In this powerful and profound book, Michael Mitton shows how it is, in fact, an essential part of both personal development and spiritual renewal. Drawing on his own experience of the 'homecoming' journey, he considers how we can go about finding our true home within God's eternal kingdom, how to identify the forces within us that may hinder this search, and the importance of churches offering a welcoming home to all.

Each chapter concludes with questions for personal reflection or group discussion and the book also features an imaginative retelling of the parable of the prodigal son, addressing some of the issues raised through a story-based approach.

ISBN 978 1 84101 877 5   £7.99
Available from your local Christian bookshop or, in case of difficulty, direct from BRF: please visit www.brfonline.org.uk.

Also available for Kindle

Enjoyed
this book?

Write a review—we'd love to hear what you think.
Email: reviews@brf.org.uk

Keep up to date—receive details of our new books as they happen.
Sign up for email news and select your interest groups at:
www.brfonline.org.uk/findoutmore/

Follow us on Twitter @brfonline

By post—to receive new title information by post (UK only), complete
the form below and post to: BRF Mailing Lists, 15 The Chambers, Vineyard,
Abingdon, Oxfordshire, OX14 3FE

Your Details
Name
Address
Town/City _____ Post Code _____
Email

Your Interest Groups (*Please tick as appropriate)	
☐ Advent/Lent	☐ Messy Church
☐ Bible Reading & Study	☐ Pastoral
☐ Children's Books	☐ Prayer & Spirituality
☐ Discipleship	☐ Resources for Children's Church
☐ Leadership	☐ Resources for Schools

Support your local bookshop
Ask about their new title information schemes.

Rhythms of Grace

Finding intimacy with God in a busy life

Tony Horsfall

Rhythms of Grace emerges from a personal exploration of contemplative spirituality. Coming from an evangelical and charismatic background, Tony Horsfall felt an increasing desire to know God more deeply. At the same time, he felt an increasing dissatisfaction with his own spiritual life, as well as concern at the number of highly qualified and gifted people involved in Christian ministry who experience burn-out.

In this book he shows how contemplative spirituality, with its emphasis on realising our identity as God's beloved children and on being rather than doing, has vital lessons for us about discovering intimacy with God. It also provides essential insights about building a ministry that is both enjoyable and sustainable.

ISBN 978 1 84101 842 3   £7.99
Available from your local Christian bookshop or direct from BRF: visit www.brfonline.org.uk

Also available for Kindle.